Cooking Close to Home

A Year of Seasonal Recipes

Diane Imrie & Richard Jarmusz

with photos by Andrew Wellman

Chelsea Green Publishing

White River Junction, Vermont

Cooking Close to Home was previously
published in 2009 by the authors.

Designed by Serena Fox Design.

Prepared food photographs by Andrew Wellman.
Photos on pages 131, 158–159, 184–185, 216–217, and 230 by Pierre Levac.
Photo on page 120 supplied by Charleen Rotax.
Photo on page 235 supplied by Jericho Settlers' Farm.
Other photos by the authors.

Printed in the United States of America.
First Chelsea Green printing January, 2011.
10 9 8 7 6 5 4 3 2 1   11 12 13 14 15

green press INITIATIVE

Chelsea Green Publishing is committed to preserving
ancient forests and natural resources. We elected to
print this title on FSC®-certified paper containing at
least 10% postconsumer recycled fiber, processed
chlorine-free. As a result, for this printing, we have
saved:

14 Trees (40' tall and 6-8" diameter)
6,618 Gallons of Wastewater
5 million BTUs Total Energy
402 Pounds of Solid Waste
1,374 Pounds of Greenhouse Gases

Chelsea Green Publishing made this paper choice
because we are a member of the Green Press Initiative,
a nonprofit program dedicated to supporting authors,
publishers, and suppliers in their efforts to reduce their
use of fiber obtained from endangered forests. For more
information, visit www.greenpressinitiative.org.

Environmental impact estimates were made using the Environmental
Defense Paper Calculator. For more information visit: www
.papercalculator.org.

FSC
www.fsc.org
MIX
Paper from
responsible sources
FSC® C101537

"This book contains less than 1% of
material that is not FSC certified"

Our Commitment to Green Publishing
Chelsea Green sees publishing as a tool for cultural change and ecological stewardship. We strive to align
our book manufacturing practices with our editorial mission and to reduce the impact of our business
enterprise in the environment. We print our books and catalogs on chlorine-free recycled paper, using
vegetable-based inks whenever possible. This book may cost slightly more because it was printed
on paper that contains recycled fiber, and we hope you'll agree that it's worth it. Chelsea Green is a
member of the Green Press Initiative (www.greenpressinitiative.org), a nonprofit coalition of publishers,
manufacturers, and authors working to protect the world's endangered forests and conserve natural
resources. *Cooking Close to Home* was printed on FSC®-certified paper supplied by RR Donnelley that
contains at least 10% postconsumer recycled fiber.

Library of Congress Cataloging-in-Publication Data
Imrie, Diane.
 Cooking close to home : a year of seasonal recipes / Diane Imrie & Richard Jarmusz ; with photos by Andrew Wellman.
   p. cm.
 Includes index.
 ISBN 978-1-60358-334-3
 1. Cooking, American. I. Jarmusz, Richard. II. Title.

TX715.I347 2011
641.5973--dc22

2010050831

Chelsea Green Publishing Company
Post Office Box 428
White River Junction, VT 05001
(802) 295-6300
www.chelseagreen.com

GIVING THANKS

We give thanks to those who have joined us at our harvest table, either for just a moment or many times during the last three years.

Thanks to Dawna Jarmusz and Mike Imrie, for their commitment, constant support, encouragement, honest feedback and for enduring endless taste-testing.

Andrew Wellman, for the long days of work, excellent and unusual photography, and an enlightening experience.

Serena Fox, for her talent, enthusiasm and beautiful design work.

Deborah Shapiro, for her inspiring words.

Sharyn Duffey, for patiently editing our work.

Pete Levac, for outdoor photography.

Tony Jarmusz, for inspired editing.

Diane Jarmusz, for editing our words.

David and Paula White, for all those last minute ingredients.

Claire St-Martin, Eric Vandal and Jean Miller, for sharing family traditions.

Mike Noble, for pointing us in the right direction.

All of our friends and family that surround us each day, who gave us their impromptu support and words of wisdom.

To our farmers, for sharing their life's work with us:

Christa Alexander and Mark Fasching, from Jericho Settlers' Farm

Bill Shur, from Champlain Orchards

Hank Bissell, from Lewis Creek Farm

Paul Mazza's Fruit & Vegetable Stand

Sam Mazza's Farm Market, Bakery and Greenhouses

Allenholm Farm

Neil Sands, for sharing the honey harvest

Lastly, to Jason Frishman for supplying Master Sauce

Jeremy Ayers Pottery

Robert Kirigin and Hunger Mountain Cooperative

FOREWORD

So often when I'm planning and preparing a meal for my family, I wish that I had the wisdom of a registered dietitian and the kitchen skills of a professional chef. I imagine myself taking the freshest and healthiest ingredients, designing a nutritious and tasty menu and then preparing each recipe effortlessly and presenting it with a flourish to rave reviews.

All of this may now be within my reach thanks to Diane Imrie and Chef Richard Jarmusz. Colleagues in their professional endeavors, Diane and Richard became collaborators when they discovered their shared passion for cooking seasonally with foods purchased at local farmers' markets or grown in their own backyard.

Diane is a registered dietitian and the Director of Nutrition Services for the largest hospital system in Vermont. Richard is an accomplished executive chef and graduate of the Culinary Institute of America in Hyde Park, New York. Together, they have implemented a local and sustainable food program that serves over 5,000 meals a day to a broad and varied audience. Although their work affords them the opportunity to make a significant impact, and influence how a large number of people relate to food, they wanted to take their passion a step further.

It wasn't uncommon for Richard and Diane's Friday afternoon conversations to include a discussion about what they hoped to find at that weekend's farmers' market, and the meals they planned to prepare. Monday mornings they would review menus, exchange recipes, offer enhancements and share resources. It was only a matter of time before the concept for *Cooking Close to Home* took shape and both authors were spending their evenings and weekends writing recipes, testing dishes and listing hints and techniques that had become second nature throughout the years. All of these are now available to us in this exciting new book.

Just as I wish for some guidance in the kitchen, a shopping companion at the market would be welcome as well. That, too, is within reach. Just as an effective coach challenges you to enter unexplored territory and face your fears, Diane and Richard introduce their readers to many foods that are less popular or unfamiliar. By providing recipes that make the previously unimaginable delicious, they encourage us to taste new varieties, explore the spice rack and expand our comfort zone. Their seasonal guide to the farmers' market and the unexpected contents of a weekly farm share are informative and inspiring.

Cooking Close to Home is an ideal companion for any season. With it as your guide, you can be assured that your family and friends will soon be enjoying nourishing, delicious meals inspired by seasonal ingredients and your environment. Some wishes do come true.

Deborah Schapiro
Publisher, Edible Green Mountains

"Good food is a story,

best told at the dinner table."

CONTENTS

COOKING CLOSE TO HOME

In *Cooking Close to Home* we hope to share not just our favorite recipes but our passion for finding and cooking fresh, local and seasonal foods. Finding fresh food is an adventure, and cooking seasonally requires some creativity as we adapt our recipes depending on the harvest. It also means some effort in planning and preparation, but the rewards are so satisfying. Our recipes and Harvest Hints show you how to transition to buying foods that are simple, fresh and in season all year round. The recipes also high-light the unique varieties and flavors that are found locally and seasonally in the Northeast. Because eating fresh, unprocessed food simply means better nutrition, we share how to store the harvest when it is at its peak of freshness. These foods will nourish your heart and soul, all winter long.

There is no comparison to the satisfaction of coming home from the farmers' market with a basket full of fresh, local foods. We encourage you to take every opportunity to be engaged with your food, whether it be shaking hands with a farmer at the market, or signing up for an entire season of fresh food through a farm share. Our food system is complicated and there is a lot to learn if we want to be conscious about what we eat. Learn about your food and how it was grown—is it organic, grass-fed, raised without hormones and antibiotics? We believe that eating fresh and in season is essential to our health, to the prosperity and viability of our local farmers and to the sustainability of our planet. Cooking and eating fresh and seasonal foods that are grown by small producers in our own commu-nities reduces our carbon footprint, broadens our appreciation and aware-ness of our local growers and encourages us to develop a culture of food that has been lost in many families. As you prepare and savor local foods you are building traditions for the next generation. We are certain that many of our recipes will become your family favorites in seasons to come.

We hope that this cookbook will inspire you to think about your food, about where it comes from and why you eat it. We know that you will find hours of pleasure in the kitchen, enjoying the many delicious flavors that local foods provide!

HARVEST BEGINNINGS

Harvest Beginnings are the perfect place to start learning how to use ingredients that are fresh and simple. We chose to use fresh vegetables as the focal point for all of the following recipes, so it is easy to follow the seasons using the produce that you find at your local markets or in your own garden. With just a small amount of meat or cheese added to some of the recipes, they are a light and healthy beginning to any meal.

harvest beginnings

Prosciutto-Wrapped Asparagus with Goat Cheese and Mushroom Salad

12 to 16 asparagus stalks,
  trimmed and peeled

4 slices Prosciutto ham, sliced thin

1 ½ cups baby greens

4 portions of Mushroom Salad
  (see recipe on page 16)

4 slices goat cheese, 1 ounce each

Fresh ground black pepper

Serves four

◆ Fill a small saucepan halfway with water and bring to a boil. Add the asparagus and poach quickly, cooking about 3 minutes so that the asparagus are cooked al dente.

◆ Remove from heat and submerge the asparagus into a bath of cold water and ice. Place on a towel and pat dry.

◆ Place one slice of Prosciutto on a flat surface. Place 3 to 4 asparagus stalks on the outer edge of the ham, and roll the ham around the asparagus. Repeat with the other 3 slices of ham.

◆ On each serving plate arrange a small bed of greens in the center. Arrange the asparagus bundle on top of greens, and garnish with mushroom salad. Add a slice of goat cheese on top of or leaning on the asparagus. Season with freshly ground black pepper. Serve.

HARVEST HINT

You can find all of the fresh vegetables for this dish at the earliest spring farmers' markets, but certainly asparagus in season is a fleeting treat. Plan to cook and eat it often when it is available locally, as the taste of imported asparagus just does not compare!

MUSHROOM SALAD

¼ cup olive oil

1 cup shiitake mushrooms, sliced

1 ½ cups portabella mushrooms, sliced

1 teaspoon fresh garlic, chopped

2 tablespoons fresh basil, chopped

¼ cup balsamic vinegar

Fresh ground black pepper

Serves four

◆ Heat a medium sauté pan over medium heat. Add 1 tablespoon of olive oil, then add the mushrooms and garlic and sauté until just tender.

◆ Add the basil and continue to cook for 1 minute. Add 1 tablespoon of balsamic vinegar and stir all ingredients to mix.

◆ Remove from heat. Place the mushrooms in a bowl, add the remaining olive oil and vinegar, and mix. Season with pepper. Refrigerate until chilled.

◆ Mix lightly before serving.

HARVEST HINT

This very simple salad can be served in many different ways. Try it served with grilled steak, toss with hot or cold pasta or serve on an antipasti platter beside some fine local cheeses.

Spring Snap Peas
with Sesame Dipping Sauce

1 tablespoon honey

1 tablespoon soy sauce

1 tablespoon fresh ginger, chopped

2 teaspoons sesame oil

½ teaspoon fresh garlic, chopped

3 cups fresh snap peas,
   ends trimmed off

Fresh lemon juice

Serves four to six

◆ To make the sauce, in a small bowl combine the honey, soy sauce, ginger, sesame oil and garlic. Set aside.

◆ Heat a medium sauté pan over medium-high heat. Add the snap peas and lemon juice, and cook for 2 to 3 minutes or until just softened.

◆ Serve on a small tray with the sauce in a dipping bowl.

HARVEST HINT

Serve this appetizer when snap peas are abundant and super-sweet. It is a great way to offer vegetables before the meal is served, and is light enough that it won't ruin anyone's appetite. We suggest that you make the sauce ahead and quickly cook the peas outdoors on the grill, while relaxing on the deck with a cold drink.

Simmered Mushroom Trio
with Garlic Crostini

1 teaspoon dried porcini mushrooms,
   broken into small pieces

¼ cup dry white wine

1 tablespoon olive oil

½ medium onion, chopped

2 teaspoons all-purpose flour

1 clove garlic, chopped

2 ½ cups assorted mushrooms, sliced
   (may include crimini, shiitake, oyster,
   portabella or any other local
   mushrooms)

½ teaspoon Italian seasoning

¼ Basic Chicken Stock
   (see recipe on page 61)

1 clove garlic, cut in half

½ baguette, cut into thin slices

Olive oil for drizzling

Serves four

◆ In a small bowl soak the dried porcini mushrooms in the white wine for 15 minutes.

◆ In a medium sauté pan heat the olive oil over medium-high heat, add the onions and sauté for approximately 5 minutes, or until soft. Add the flour, stirring to coat the onions, and cook for 2 minutes.

◆ Add the chopped garlic and sauté another 30 seconds. Add the assorted mushrooms and Italian seasoning and cook for 10 minutes.

◆ Add the stock and wine with soaked mushrooms, and continue to cook another 5 minutes, until most of the liquid has evaporated.

◆ Rub the cut garlic clove on one side of each baguette slice. Toast the slices under the broiler for 5 minutes, or until slightly crisp and just browned. Place on individual plates, and drizzle with olive oil.

◆ Pour the mushroom mixture on top of the bread slices, and serve.

HARVEST HINT

Mushrooms are actually not a vegetable, but are fungi. Mushrooms have a lot to offer nutritionally—they are low in calories, and rich in selenium and ergothionine (both antioxidants). Once exposed to sunlight, mushrooms are also an unexpected source of vitamin D. Store mushrooms in the refrigerator in a paper bag, and rinse only when ready to use. Local producers are now growing mushrooms throughout the year, so indulge in whatever varieties are available.

GARLIC-ROASTED CHERRY TOMATOES WITH FRESH BASIL AND GOAT CHEESE

2 pints of cherry tomatoes

¼ cup olive oil

1 tablespoon fresh garlic, chopped

½ cup fresh basil leaves, chopped

Salt and fresh ground black
   pepper, to taste

Small whole-wheat baguette

4 ounces goat cheese

Serves four

◆ Preheat the grill to low, approximately 250 °F.

◆ In a heavy stainless steel saucepan, stir together the tomatoes, olive oil and garlic.

◆ Cook this slowly on the grill for approximately 45 minutes, or until all the tomatoes have burst. The sauce should be slightly thickened when ready.

◆ Stir in the fresh basil, salt and pepper.

◆ Slice the baguette lengthwise and toast on the grill. Lightly spread on your favorite goat cheese, and top generously with garlic-roasted cherry tomatoes. Serve.

HARVEST HINT

This recipe can be served as an appetizer, or as a light main dish served with a green salad. This is also delicious served as a sauce over fresh, homemade pasta. Sauce can be stored in the freezer for up to three months.

Cucumber Boats with Fiery Beef

Boats

1 large cucumber

2 tablespoons rice vinegar

1 teaspoon Thai fish sauce

½ teaspoon tarragon leaves, chopped

Fiery beef

1 teaspoon canola oil

½ cup (raw) top round beef,
   finely shredded

½ cup carrots, shredded

½ cup red bell pepper, matchstick sliced

½ teaspoon fresh garlic, finely chopped

½ teaspoon fresh ginger, finely chopped

½ teaspoon dried hot chiles, ground

½ teaspoon paprika

½ cup Basic Chicken Stock
   (see page on 61 page)

1 tablespoon soy sauce

Micro greens, to garnish

Serves Six

◆ Peel the cucumber and slice in half lengthwise. Using a spoon, hollow out the seeds to form a boat. Cut into pieces that are 1 ½ inches long.

◆ In a medium bowl add the rice vinegar, fish sauce and tarragon, and whisk until blended. Add the cucumbers and toss until coated. Set aside.

◆ In a sauté pan add the canola oil and heat over medium-high. Add the beef and cook until it starts to brown.

◆ Add the carrots, pepper, garlic, ginger and chiles, and continue to cook for 2 to 4 minutes, stirring frequently. Add the paprika and stir into beef mixture.

◆ Stir in the chicken stock and the soy sauce. Cook until most of the liquid has evaporated and the beef is coated but still moist. Remove from heat and let cool for 5 minutes.

◆ Place the cucumber boats on a serving platter and fill each with about 1 tablespoon of beef mixture. Top each cucumber half with a small amount of micro greens. Serve or refrigerate for later use.

EGGPLANT AND FIELD TOMATO TAPENADE

2 tablespoons olive oil

4 teaspoons fresh garlic, finely chopped

½ cup onion, finely chopped

½ cup green bell pepper, finely chopped

1 ½ cups eggplant,
   chopped quarter-inch

1 cup fresh tomato, finely chopped,
   saving any juice

¼ cup Fresh Tomato Juice
   (see recipe on page 43)

1 tablespoon balsamic vinegar

1 tablespoon fresh basil, finely chopped

1 tablespoon fresh oregano, chopped

Salt and fresh ground black pepper,
   to taste

Serves six

◆ Heat olive oil in a medium sauté pan. Add the garlic and onion and sauté over medium heat for 3 to 4 minutes, or until onions are tender. Add the bell pepper and eggplant and sauté for 5 more minutes.

◆ Add the tomato and any juices, tomato juice, vinegar, basil, oregano, salt and black pepper, and mix well.

◆ Reduce heat and simmer for 15 minutes or until thickened.

◆ Place in bowl and serve with sliced baguettes, pita chips or crisps. This tapenade may be served hot or cold.

HARVEST HINT

This dip can be used in place of the store-bought version, which is often higher in sodium. To keep the sodium lower in this homemade recipe, add just a pinch of salt at the end of preparation.

SPICY TURKEY PASTRIES WITH CILANTRO AND LIME

1 teaspoon olive oil

½ pound ground turkey

1 cup zucchini, finely chopped

¼ cup onion, finely chopped

¼ cup green bell pepper, finely chopped

2 teaspoons garlic, chopped

1 teaspoon jalapeño pepper,
   finely chopped

1 teaspoon paprika

½ cup Basic Chicken Stock
   (see recipe on page 61)

2 tablespoons lime juice

1 tablespoon tomato paste

¼ teaspoon salt

2 tablespoons cilantro, finely chopped

Chipotle Flour Tortilla recipe
   (see recipe on page 27)

Serves six

◆ Heat a skillet over medium heat. Add the olive oil and turkey, and sauté until browned.

◆ Add the zucchini, onions, bell peppers, garlic and jalapeño pepper and sauté for 3 to 5 minutes, until vegetables just begin to soften. Add paprika and sauté for 2 more minutes.

◆ Add the chicken stock, lime juice, tomato paste and salt, and stir to mix well. Cook until the liquid is reduced to a thick sauce consistency. Add the cilantro and stir until blended. Remove from heat and set aside.

TO MAKE THE PASTRY

◆ Preheat the oven to 375 °F.

◆ Cut the Chipotle Flour Tortilla dough into 6 pieces and roll out so that dough forms 4-inch long logs. Let the dough rest for 5 minutes.

◆ With a pasta machine, work the dough through the wringer until you reach the third-lowest level. The dough should form a sheet like a lasagna noodle. Cut into 4-inch by 4-inch squares.

◆ Divide the filling equally on each square. Fold over into a triangle, and crimp with the tip of a fork, pinching the dough together.

◆ Place on a lightly greased baking sheet and bake in the oven for 10 to 12 minutes, until lightly browned and firm. Remove from the oven and serve.

FRESH TOMATO BRUSCHETTA

3 cups fresh tomatoes, chopped

½ cup red onion, finely chopped

¼ cup fresh basil, chopped

2 tablespoons fresh garlic, minced

1 tablespoon red wine vinegar

1 tablespoon balsamic vinegar

¼ cup olive oil

Bruschetta

3 tablespoons olive oil

2 tablespoons fresh garlic, minced

1 (16-ounce) Parisian bread or baguette,
   sliced into ¼-inch slices

Serves six to eight

◆ In a medium bowl combine the tomatoes, onion and basil, and mix together.

◆ In a small bowl combine the garlic, vinegars and olive oil, and whisk together. Pour over the tomato mixture and mix well.

◆ In a small bowl combine the olive oil and garlic and mix well. Brush the oil mixture onto one side of each slice of bread.

◆ To make the bruschetta, use either your grill or broiler to toast the bread until lightly browned.

◆ Serve the tomato mixture in a bowl, surrounded by the toasted bread on a platter, and let your guests top their own bruschettas.

HARVEST HINT

The term bruschetta means "to roast over coals". The traditional way to make bruschetta is to rub sliced bread with fresh garlic and drizzle with olive oil, then grill over hot coals. Tomato dishes are best made with fresh tomatoes, hot off the vine. We encourage you to eat fresh tomatoes only when they are local and in season. Plan ahead and preserve tomatoes yourself for the rest of the year.

NOTE FROM RICHARD—
I take monthly trips to Portland, Maine, to visit family and friends, and this has given me the opportunity to stop and visit many local markets along the way. It is a great place to meet farmers from different areas and learn about what they grow or produce, and you never know what surprise ingredients you will find. One of my favorite discoveries is the farmers' market in Portland on Saturday. This is one of the biggest in the Northeast; there are more than 30 farms and vendors selling local produce, cheese, fruit, meats and flowers. The market is set up on the north side of Deering Oaks Park and the street is lined with vendors. There are crowds of people and there is always a musician or two playing, creating a fun and festive atmosphere. This Saturday ritual always includes our dog, who leads us through the market. There are many stops along the way to receive an occasional treat, all the while juggling bags full of local harvest. We plan to get to the market early in the morning when the produce is piled high and choices are plentiful. When we have arrived later in the afternoon we have found the choices and quality to be more limited. So remember, the early localvore gets the best root.

HARVEST HINT

WHEN PLANNING A TRIP, take the time to find farmers' markets in the city or town where you are going. All State Department of Agriculture websites list the day and times of local farmers' markets.

GRILLED CORN AND BEAN SALSA
WITH CHIPOTLE TORTILLA CHIPS

2 ears corn on the cob, not husked

1 cup dried black beans, cooked

2 cups fresh tomato, seeded, chopped

½ cup onion, finely chopped

½ cup green or red bell pepper,

 finely chopped

¼ cup fresh cilantro, chopped

1 teaspoon chili powder

2 tablespoons fresh garlic, chopped

¼ cup red wine vinegar

¼ teaspoon kosher salt

2 tablespoons fresh jalapeño pepper,

 finely chopped

Chipotle Tortilla Chips

 (see recipe on page 27)

Makes approximately five cups of salsa

◆ Preheat the grill to medium heat (approximately 350 °F). Remove most of the silk from the corn, leaving the husk still on. Grill for about 20 minutes, until the corn begins to lightly brown. Remove from the grill and let cool. Husk the corn, and cut off the kernels.

◆ In a medium bowl combine the corn, beans, tomato, onion, bell pepper, cilantro, chili powder, garlic, vinegar, salt and jalapeño and mix well. If you like a milder salsa, use a little less jalapeño. This recipe can be made a day ahead and refrigerated. Serve with Chipotle Tortilla Chips.

HARVEST HINT

This salsa is robust in flavor, low-fat and high in fiber.
Use this salsa to spice up a sandwich wrap, grilled chicken or beef, or toss it into a salad.

Chipotle Flour Tortillas and Tortilla Chips

1 cup all-purpose flour

1 tablespoon cornmeal

¼ cup plus 2 tablespoons water

¼ teaspoon salt

½ teaspoon chipotle powder

½ teaspoon paprika

1 teaspoon olive oil

Makes eight tortillas

◆ In a mixing bowl combine the flour, cornmeal, water, salt, chipotle powder, paprika and olive oil. Using a dough hook, mix on low speed until a ball forms. Remove from bowl, cover and let the dough rest for 1 hour.

◆ Divide the dough into 8 pieces and roll each piece to ⅛-inch thickness. You can also use a pasta machine to roll out the dough, rolling out until you reach the thinnest setting on your machine. The shape of the dough will be oblong, not round.

◆ Let tortillas rest for 15 minutes.

◆ Cook in a skillet or griddle on medium heat, about 2 minutes each side. They are now ready to stuff with your favorite filling.

TO MAKE TORTILLA CHIPS

◆ Follow steps 1 through 3 above.

◆ Preheat the oven to 375 °F.

◆ Cut each of the rolled dough into wedges, about 8 per piece of dough.

◆ Place the wedges on a cookie sheet and bake in the oven for 9 to 10 minutes until crisp. Remove from the oven and let cool.

Lamb and Pumpkin Quesadilla
with Cilantro Sour Cream

1 teaspoon olive oil

8 ounces ground lamb

¼ cup onion, chopped

2 teaspoons fresh garlic, chopped

1 ¼ cup raw pumpkin, shredded

3 tablespoons fresh cilantro, chopped

2 tablespoons water

¼ teaspoon dried ground
   chipotle pepper

⅛ teaspoon salt

4 ounces cheddar cheese, shredded

6 six-inch whole-wheat tortillas

Olive oil for pan

1 cup sour cream

2 tablespoons fresh cilantro, chopped

Serves eight

◆ Heat a large sauté pan over medium heat. Add olive oil, ground lamb, onion and garlic, and sauté until fully cooked. Stir to crumble lamb as it is cooking.

◆ Add the pumpkin, cilantro, water, chipotle pepper and salt, and sauté for 3 to 5 minutes until pumpkin is tender but still holds its shape.

◆ Remove from heat. Place the lamb mixture in a bowl and mix in the cheddar cheese.

◆ Lay out the tortillas and divide the filling equally between them.

◆ Spread filling on one half and fold over to form a half moon.

◆ Heat a large sauté pan over medium heat and lightly oil. Place the filled tortillas in pan and cook about two minutes on each side.

◆ In a small bowl mix together the sour cream and cilantro.

◆ Cut each tortilla into 3 triangles and serve with cilantro sour cream on the side.

HARVEST HINT

Many people think of pumpkin as a decoration that sits on the front porch in October. Pumpkin is the largest fruit grown in New England, and is a colorful ingredient that is extremely versatile. A unique and practical way to include pumpkin in a meal is by grating it fresh, as we do in this recipe, or by chopping or slicing it finely, so that it cooks quickly. The long baking time required for pumpkin purée can get in the way of a quick meal, but using fresh pumpkin is quick and delicious.

Spicy Tomato Verde
with Multigrain Crisps

½ cup dried cherry tomatoes

1 teaspoon olive oil

3 ounces cream cheese

1 tablespoon lime juice

¼ teaspoon dried hot pepper

1 cup tomatillos, peeled and halved

2 tablespoons fresh cilantro

2 cloves garlic

¼ cup red onion, sliced

Multigrain Crisps (see recipe
  on page 157)

Equipment Needed

5-inch springform pan

Serves six

◆ In a small bowl, toss the dried tomatoes with the olive oil and let soak for 60 minutes.

◆ Spread the cream cheese in the bottom of a 5-inch springform pan.

◆ In a food processor, combine the soaked tomatoes with olive oil, lime juice and dried hot pepper, and process until it is finely minced. Spread the tomato mixture on top of the cheese.

◆ In a food processor, combine the tomatillos, cilantro, garlic and red onion and roughly chop. Layer this mixture on top of the tomato layer.

◆ Cover and refrigerate at least 2 hours. To serve, remove the sides of the springform pan. Serve with Multigrain Crisps.

HARVEST HINT

Tomatillos are a fruit that is in the tomato family and is actually grown similarly to a tomato. To store, pull the whole plant and hang in a cool, dry, dark place. When ready to use, remove the husk and wash the fruit. Tomatillos are a very good source of vitamin C.

Savory Apple Cheddar Turnovers

1 teaspoon olive oil

⅓ cup onion, chopped

1 cup fresh McIntosh apple, chopped

½ cup sharp cheddar cheese, shredded

1 carrot, peeled and minced in
   a food processor (enough
   to make ½ cup minced)

1 teaspoon dried parsley

1 tablespoon Homegrown Horseradish
   (see recipe on page 229)

⅛ teaspoon salt

⅛ teaspoon fresh ground black pepper

8 sheets phyllo dough, thawed

Olive oil for dough

Makes twelve turnovers

◆ Preheat the oven to 425 ºF.

◆ Heat a small sauté pan over medium heat. Add the olive oil and onion, and cook for 7 minutes or until slightly browned.

◆ In a medium bowl combine the onions, apple, cheese, carrots, parsley, horseradish, salt and pepper, and mix well.

◆ While working with the phyllo dough, keep it covered with plastic wrap and a damp dish cloth. Remove one sheet of dough and lay it on a clean surface. Brush lightly with olive oil. Layer another sheet on top and brush lightly again with olive oil. Using a pizza cutter cut the dough into thirds width-wise. Add 1 heaping tablespoon of the mixture to the corner of one strip, and fold into a triangle. Continue folding until you reach the end of the strip. Repeat. Place on a cookie sheet.

◆ Bake for 10 minutes and serve immediately. If making ahead, wrap tightly and bake just before serving.

HARVEST HINT

The number of local farmstead and artisan cheese producers is increasing, and so their fine cheeses have become more widely available. There are so many different varieties to try that it is almost impossible to pick a favorite. There is a seasonal component to cheese, depending on what is growing in the fields at the time that the goats, cows or sheep are milked. Depending on what the animals have been grazing on, the flavor of the cheese can vary so that even your favorite cheese might have a different taste from season to season and from year to year.

Garden Fries
with Garlicky Leek Dipping Sauce

Fries

1 pound of fall vegetables
(may include carrots, parsnips, turnip,
potatoes, rutabaga), washed, peeled,
and cut ¼-inch by ¼-inch, 3 inches long

1 tablespoon olive oil

⅛ teaspoon ground red pepper

⅛ teaspoon garlic powder

½ teaspoon Worcestershire sauce

Dipping sauce

1 leek, sliced in half lengthwise
and cut into 1-inch pieces

1 tablespoon olive oil

2 garlic cloves, baked

1 teaspoon dried parsley

1 cup low fat sour cream

Serves four

◆ Preheat oven to 450 ºF.

◆ In a large bowl combine the sliced fall vegetables, olive oil, red pepper, garlic powder and Worcestershire and toss to coat well.

◆ Lay the vegetables out on a baking sheet, in a single layer.

◆ Bake for 30 minutes, turning once.

◆ Soak the chopped leek in water for 10 minutes. Drain and rinse.

◆ In a small sauté pan heat the olive oil over medium. Add the leek and cook until softened and slightly browned, approximately 5 minutes. Let the leeks cool completely before proceeding to the next step.

◆ Combine the leek, olive oil, garlic, parsley and sour cream in a food processor, and mix until smoothly blended. Place in a bowl and refrigerate. The leek dipping sauce can be prepared several hours ahead.

◆ Serve the fries hot with dipping sauce on the side.

HARVEST HINT

Root vegetables are a staple in the Northeastern winter, and a large component of any winter farm share. This recipe is very useful when you have a variety of root vegetables, and are looking for something a little different to do with them that the kids will enjoy. This recipe can be served as an appetizer or as part of a main meal. The dipping sauce also makes an excellent topping for fresh baked potatoes.

Root vegetables
are a staple in the
Northeastern winter,
and a large component of
any winter farm share.

THE LOCALVORE MOVEMENT is committed to local, sustainable food within a community. A localvore is usually considered to be someone who eats food produced within a defined distance from where they live (often within a 100-mile radius). To a localvore, the Marco Polo exception means that salt and exotic spices can be used in your cooking, even though they are not produced locally. *Garden Fries* is a perfect recipe for a committed localvore!

SPROUTS ARE BECOMING MORE WIDELY AVAILABLE at winter farmers' markets, and add a
fresh green taste and texture to winter dishes. If you want to grow your own, sprouting trays are fairly inexpensive
to buy and are easy to use, providing fresh sprouts at an economical price. If you cannot find sunflower sprouts you
can substitute with pea greens in this recipe.

VERMONT VEGETABLE
NEW YEAR ROLLS

Egg rolls

1 tablespoon olive oil

1 tablespoon fresh garlic, chopped

2 cups red cabbage, sliced

1 cup carrots, chopped

1 cup celeriac or celery,
  peeled and chopped

3 ounces sunflower sprouts

1 green onion, chopped

2 tablespoons fresh cilantro, chopped

1 package egg roll dough or wrappers
  (about 1 pound or 20 wrappers)

Olive oil for pan

Sauce

1 teaspoon olive oil

1 tablespoon fresh garlic, finely chopped

1 tablespoon fresh ginger,
  finely chopped

1 teaspoon cornstarch

⅓ cup orange juice

1 tablespoon low-sodium soy sauce

1 tablespoon honey

1 teaspoon sesame oil

Makes twelve turnovers

◆ Heat a large sauté pan over medium heat. Add the olive oil, garlic, cabbage, carrots and celeriac, and sauté for approximately 10 minutes; vegetables should still be firm. Remove from heat and let cool until you are able to handle the mixture.

◆ Add the sprouts, onion and cilantro to the pan and mix well.

◆ Lay out four egg roll sheets at a time. Add a generous ¼-cup of mixture to each piece of egg roll dough, and roll following the instructions on the package. Cover and set aside until all are complete.

◆ To cook the egg rolls, add enough olive oil to lightly cover the bottom of a sauté pan. Heat over medium-high heat, and when oil is thoroughly heated, add egg rolls. Turn the egg rolls frequently and cook for 10 minutes, or until roll is consistently lightly browned.

◆ To make the sauce, add the olive oil, garlic and ginger to a small sauté pan, and cook over medium heat for 1 minute.

◆ Whisk the cornstarch into the orange juice and add to the sauté pan. Add the soy sauce, honey and sesame oil and continue to cook for approximately 2 minutes, or until sauce is thickened. Sauce can be prepared ahead and refigerated. Serve the egg rolls on a platter with the sauce in a small bowl.

SEASONAL SOUPS

When you think about comfort food it is often homemade soup that comes to mind. It's the wonderful smell that fills the house on a cold winter day, or the chilled soup that helps you cool off on a lazy summer afternoon. There are two important components to consider when making soup: high quality stock and fresh, seasonal ingredients.

Homemade stock is essential, so we have included a Basic Chicken Stock recipe that is used in many of the soups; or if you prefer you can use your own vegetarian stock recipe as a substitute. The basic ingredients used to make stock are generally available year-round, so it is easy to make and keep stock on hand in the freezer for any season.

It is the addition of fresh, seasonal vegetables that make soups an interesting addition to the table all year. For more variety we encourage you to follow our Harvest Hints for substituting seasonal vegetables in some of the recipes. Make a pot of soup, add a salad and bread, and you will have a quick, simple and satisfying meal anytime of year.

seasonal soups

WINTER

HOT AND SOUR SPINACH
AND DANDELION GREENS SOUP

1 tablespoon butter

3 cloves fresh garlic or 3 fresh
  garlic scapes, chopped

½ cup fresh chives, chopped

¼ teaspoon white pepper

¼ teaspoon crushed red pepper flakes

3 cups Basic Chicken Stock (see recipe
  on page 61)

1 tablespoon cornstarch

1 tablespoon sesame oil

1 tablespoon honey

1 teaspoon lemon juice

2 cups fresh spinach, chopped

2 cups fresh dandelion greens, chopped

3 tablespoons rice wine vinegar

1 whole egg

Serves four

◆ In a soup pot melt the butter over medium-high heat.
Add the garlic or garlic scapes and chives, and sauté for 2 to
3 minutes until the chives are wilted. Add the white pepper,
crushed red pepper flakes and 2 ½ cups of the stock, reserving
½ cup of stock. Bring to a boil.

◆ Thoroughly mix the cornstarch into the reserved
½ cup of stock. Add 1 ladle of the hot soup to the stock and
cornstarch, and mix until smooth. Add this mix back to the
soup pot, stir and reduce to a simmer.

◆ In a large sauté pan, heat the sesame oil over medium-high
heat. Add the honey, lemon juice, spinach, dandelion greens
and sauté for approximately 1 minute, or until the greens are
wilted. Add the rice wine vinegar and stir.

◆ Add the spinach and dandelion mixture to the soup pot. Stir.

◆ In a small bowl lightly beat the egg. Add to the soup,
and stir gently. When the egg is cooked, remove the soup from
heat and serve.

HARVEST HINT

This is a local version of a Chinese hot and sour soup, and is a delicious way to sample dandelion greens if you are not
familiar with them. The best time of year to pick and eat dandelion greens is in the spring, when they are young
and tender.

CREAMY ASPARAGUS
BRIE SOUP

1 teaspoon olive oil

½ medium white onion, chopped

2 teaspoons fresh garlic, chopped

2 cups fresh asparagus,
   chopped into ¼-inch slices

1 cup potato, peeled and chopped

4 cups Basic Chicken Stock
   (see page 61 for recipe)

6 ounces Brie cheese

¼ teaspoon salt

¼ teaspoon fresh ground black pepper

Serves four

◆ Heat a soup pot over medium-high heat. Add the olive oil, onion and garlic, and sauté for 1 minute.

◆ Add the asparagus and potato and sauté for 2 more minutes, stirring continuously so as not to burn the vegetables.

◆ Add the stock and bring to a boil. Reduce heat and simmer for about 20 minutes, or until the potatoes are tender.

◆ Remove from heat. Using an immersion blender (or counter-top blender) blend soup ingredients until smooth. Add the Brie cheese, salt and pepper and continue to blend until smooth and creamy. Serve.

HARVEST HINT

This is a rich, creamy soup that is thickened with the potatoes. Early spring is a good time to use up any potatoes that might be left from winter storage.

Summer Gazpacho Soup
(and Fresh Tomato Juice)

1 ¼ cups Fresh Tomato Juice

   (see recipe below)

1 cup fresh tomato, finely chopped

¼ cup onion, finely chopped

½ cup green bell pepper, finely chopped

¾ cup cucumber, seeded and

   finely chopped

1 tablespoon fresh garlic, chopped

½ teaspoon hot sauce

1 tablespoon red wine vinegar

¼ teaspoon salt

Serves four

◆ In a large bowl combine the tomato juice, tomato, onion, pepper, cucumber, garlic, hot sauce, vinegar and salt, and mix well.

◆ Chill in the refrigerator for at least 2 hours before serving.

FRESH TOMATO JUICE

2 cups tomatoes, roughly chopped

½ cup water

¼ teaspoon salt

◆ In a blender combine the tomatoes, water and salt, and purée until smooth.

◆ Place the mixture in a medium saucepan and quickly bring to a boil. Boil for 2 minutes, then remove from heat and refrigerate.

HARVEST HINT

There is just no tasty alternative to freshly made tomato juice. Undoubtedly it will make the best Bloody Mary you have ever tasted!

Cold Cucumber Cream Soup with Cilantro

3 cups cucumbers, peeled,
seeded and finely chopped

⅓ cup plain yogurt

⅓ cup sour cream

¼ cup white onion, finely chopped

2 tablespoons green bell peppers,
finely chopped

½ tablespoon fresh garlic, chopped

2 tablespoons cilantro, finely chopped

¼ teaspoon fresh ground black pepper

¼ teaspoon salt

Sliced cucumber and chopped
fresh chives, for garnish

Serves four

◆ In a large bowl combine the cucumber, yogurt, sour cream, onion, peppers and garlic, and mix well.

◆ Remove 2 cups of mixture and set aside. Using an immersion blender (or countertop blender) blend soup ingredients until smooth.

◆ Combine the puréed soup and the 2 cups of reserved mixture. Add the cilantro, pepper and salt. Mix well and refrigerate for at least 60 minutes. Serve garnished with sliced cucumber and chopped chives.

HARVEST HINT

Cilantro is the leaves and stems of the coriander plant. Cilantro looks similar to Italian parsley but has a very distinctive, fresh flavor. It is used in a variety of cuisines but is often associated with Southwestern, Asian and Mexican foods. Cilantro's flavor is strong enough to stand up to hot and spicy foods, but is also a great complement to lighter dishes, like fruit salsas.

CHUNKY ROASTED TOMATO SOUP

3 tablespoons olive oil

3 ½ pounds Roma tomatoes, cored

1 cup white onion, chopped

2 teaspoons fresh garlic, chopped

4 cups Basic Chicken Stock
   (see page 61 for recipe)

½ teaspoon dried oregano

½ teaspoon dried basil

½ teaspoon dried parsley

½ teaspoon salt

¼ teaspoon fresh ground black pepper

Serves six

◆ Preheat the oven to 325 °F.

◆ Pour 1 tablespoon of oil to lightly cover the bottom of a roasting pan. Slice the tomatoes in half, and place them cut side facing upwards in pan. Make sure that the tomatoes fit snugly in the pan. Drizzle 1 tablespoon oil over the tomatoes. Bake for 2 ½ hours, until tomatoes collapse. Halfway through the cooking time, drizzle the last tablespoon of oil over the tomatoes.

◆ When the tomatoes are finished cooking, drain the pan juices into a soup pot. Add the onion and garlic to the pot and sauté for approximately 5 minutes, until the onions begin to soften.

◆ Add the tomatoes, stock, oregano, basil, parsley, salt and pepper to the soup pot, and simmer for 45 minutes. Serve.

HARVEST HINT

Tomatoes are so abundant in the summer that it can be almost overwhelming to keep up with the harvest, especially if you have your own garden. Roasting tomatoes gives them a rich, dense flavor that adds character to any recipe. This soup is a great way of preserving that roasted tomato flavor into the winter, as it freezes very well.

CREAMY LEEK AND BROCCOLI SOUP

2 tablespoons olive oil

2 cloves fresh garlic,
   peeled and chopped

2 leeks, washed and chopped

1 medium potato, peeled and chopped

3 cups broccoli, including
   stems and leaves

4 cups Basic Chicken Stock
   (see page 61 for recipe)

1 cup water

½ teaspoon dried dill

½ teaspoon fresh ground black pepper

¼ teaspoon salt

⅛ teaspoon crushed red pepper flakes

¾ cup whole milk

¼ cup crème frâiche

Garlic croutons, to garnish

Serves eight

◆ Heat the oil in a soup pot over medium-high heat. Add the garlic and leek and sauté for approximately 10 minutes or until they are wilting and soft.

◆ Add the potato and sauté for another 2 minutes.

◆ Add the broccoli, stock, water, dill, black pepper, salt and crushed red pepper and bring to a boil. Reduce heat, add the milk and simmer. Cook until the ingredients are fork tender, about 45 to 60 minutes.

◆ Remove from heat. Using an immersion blender (or countertop blender) blend soup ingredients until smooth and thickened.

◆ Return to heat. Add the crème frâiche to the soup and serve. Garnish each bowl with several garlic croutons.

HARVEST HINT

To wash leeks, cut off the roots and the top two inches of the leeks, then slice down the middle length-wise. Chop the leek into half-inch pieces. Place in a large bowl and cover with water. Using your hands, separate the layers of the leeks. Let the leeks soak in the water for five minutes to allow any sand to sink to the bottom of the bowl. Gently remove the leeks and rinse with cold water, repeating if necessary.

ROASTED FIVE-ONION SOUP

1 ½ cups leeks, washed and chopped

1 ½ cups red onion, chopped

1 cup white or yellow onion, chopped

1 cup Rio Sweet onion, chopped

4 cloves fresh garlic

1 tablespoon olive oil

2 ½ cups Basic Chicken Stock
  (see page 61 for recipe)

1 ¼ cups potato, peeled and chopped

¼ cup celeriac or celery, chopped

½ cup heavy cream

Salt and fresh ground black pepper,
  to taste

¼ cup green onion, chopped

Serves four

◆ Preheat oven to 350 °F.

◆ In a medium bowl combine the leeks, red onion, white or yellow onion, sweet onion, garlic and olive oil, and mix well. Place in a roasting pan and roast for 17 to 20 minutes in the oven, until tender and the sugars in the onions begin to caramelize.

◆ Remove the onions from the oven and place in a soup pot. Deglaze the onion pan with ½ cup of stock. Add this to the onions in the soup pot.

◆ Add the remaining stock, potato and celeriac to the soup pot and bring to a boil. Reduce heat and simmer for 25 minutes or until potatoes are tender.

◆ Remove from heat. Using an immersion blender (or countertop blender) blend soup ingredients until smooth. Return to heat, add the cream and bring to a boil.

◆ Reduce heat, add salt and pepper and add chopped green onion. Serve.

HARVEST HINT

Onions and garlic are both related to the lily family. Onions are available in different forms year-round, and are an essential storage vegetable and ingredient throughout the winter. Onions store best in a cool, dry place.

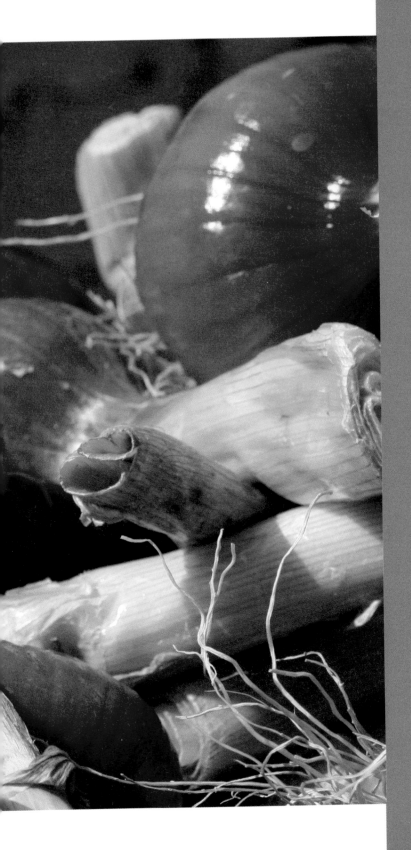

WHAT ARE...
FOOD MILES?

The term "food miles" describes how far a food has traveled before it is purchased and consumed. The higher the number of food miles, the more energy consumed to deliver that food. The average pound of produce travels 1500 miles to reach our tables, which makes food transportation a significant contributor of carbon dioxide emissions and air pollution. In fact, about 20 percent of fossil fuel use in this country goes towards the food production system. It is a simple equation: the closer to home that your food is produced, purchased and consumed, the less pollution is generated.

"Worries go down better with soup."
—Jewish Proverb

WHITE BEAN AND KALE SOUP

1 teaspoon olive oil

1 cup onions , chopped

½ cup carrots, finely chopped

½ cup celeriac or celery, finely chopped

2 teaspoons fresh garlic, chopped

½ tablespoon dried basil

4 cups Basic Chicken Stock

  (see page 61 for recipe)

  or vegetable stock

3 cups tomato, seeded and chopped

  (may use frozen as well)

3 teaspoons tomato paste

1 ½ cups white beans, cooked

1 teaspoon salt

1 teaspoon fresh ground black pepper

1 cup kale, chopped

Serves eight

◆ Heat a soup pot over medium heat and add the oil, onions, carrots, and celeriac. Cook until tender, about 4 to 6 minutes.

◆ Add the garlic and basil, and sauté for 2 more minutes.

◆ Add the stock, tomatoes and tomato paste and bring to a boil. Reduce heat and simmer for 15 minutes.

◆ Add the white beans, salt and pepper and return to a boil. Turn off heat and add the chopped kale. Mix well and serve quickly so that kale is wilted but still crisp.

HARVEST HINT

We grow our own white (or cannellini) beans because they can be difficult to find locally. One of the most common dried beans in the Northeast is the yellow eye bean, which you can use as a substitute in this recipe.

PUMPKIN CHEDDAR-ALE SOUP
(PHOTO PAGE 40)

1 teaspoon olive oil

½ cup onions, finely chopped

1 teaspoon garlic, chopped

¼ cup carrots, finely chopped

¼ cup celeriac or celery, finely chopped

3 teaspoons all-purpose flour

1 cup medium amber ale

2 cups Basic Chicken Stock

  (see page 61 for recipe)

¾ cup roasted pumpkin purée

  (see page 199 for Harvest Hint)

3 tablespoons sour cream

¼ teaspoon fresh ground black pepper

⅛ teaspoon fresh sage, minced

4 ounces sharp cheddar, finely shredded

Serves four

◆ Heat soup pot over medium heat. Add olive oil, onion, garlic, carrots and celeriac, and sauté until tender, about 4 to 6 minutes.

◆ Add flour to coat vegetables and continue to cook for 2 minutes.

◆ Stir in the ale, stock and pumpkin. Bring to a boil, then reduce heat and simmer for 10 minutes.

◆ Remove from heat. Using an immersion blender (or countertop blender) blend soup ingredients until smooth.

◆ Return to heat. Whisk in sour cream, pepper and sage. Finally, whisk in the cheddar cheese and serve.

HARVEST HINT

Beer is one of the oldest brewed beverages, dating back to the early Egyptian times. Today you can find a variety of beer flavors brewed close to home. Beer is brewed from grains, usually hops, barley or wheat, and sometimes infused with seasonal flavors like fruit or spices. Beer pairs well with local cheeses, and can be an interesting ingredient in making bread, stews, soups and marinades. You can now find local beer that is certified by the Northeast Organic Farmers Association.

CARROT
AND ROASTED FENNEL SOUP

1 bulb fennel, quartered
  and stem removed

½ large yellow onion, chopped

3 cloves garlic, peeled and sliced in half

2 tablespoons olive oil

1 pound carrots, peeled and
  cut into 1-inch pieces

1 quart Basic Chicken Stock
  (see page 61 for recipe)

¼ teaspoon dried dill

⅛ teaspoon fresh ground black pepper

¼ cup crème fraîche

Serves four

◆ Preheat the oven to 375 °F.

◆ In a small roasting pan toss the fennel, onion, garlic and oil together. Roast in the oven for 20 minutes, stirring occasionally.

◆ In a soup pot, add the roasted vegetables, carrots, stock, dill and pepper. Bring to a boil, them simmer over low heat for 35 to 45 minutes or until carrots are fork tender.

◆ Remove from heat. Using an immersion blender (or countertop blender) blend soup ingredients until smooth.

◆ Return the soup to heat and stir in the crème fraîche. Serve.

HARVEST HINT

Carrots are a staple ingredient of winter cooking in the Northeast. If you belong to a winter farm share, you know that carrots will be available until the very last pickup of the season, usually in late March. Traditionally carrots have been stored for winter in a root cellar, layered with sand. They will keep their crunch well into late spring.

HUNTER STYLE LAMB SOUP
(PHOTO PAGE 37)

1 teaspoon olive oil

4 ounces finely diced or ground lamb

½ cup fennel, chopped

⅓ cup onion, finely chopped

¼ cup celeriac or celery, finely chopped

¼ cup carrots, finely chopped

3 medium-sized garlic cloves,
   thinly sliced

3 teaspoons all-purpose flour

3 cups lamb stock or Basic Chicken Stock
   (see page 61 for recipe)

2 tablespoons cilantro, chopped

¼ teaspoon salt

⅛ teaspoon fresh ground black pepper

Serves four

◆ In a soup pot, heat oil over medium heat. Add the lamb and cook until brown, stirring frequently.

◆ Add the fennel, onion, celeriac, carrots and garlic, and sauté for 2 minutes.

◆ While stirring the vegetables, slowly add the flour to coat the vegetables,and cook for another 2 minutes.

◆ Add the stock and bring to a boil. Reduce heat and simmer for 25 minutes.

◆ Add the cilantro, salt and pepper. Serve.

HARVEST HINT

Obviously there is no hunting season for lamb, but the style of this soup inspired the name. It is chunky and uses small amounts of meat to enrich the soup. It is satisfying enough to be a main dish, and is a delicious way to use left over cooked lamb, either from a roast or other cuts.

ASIAN SPICE MUSHROOM AND KALE SOUP

1 tablespoon olive oil

1 tablespoon sesame oil

2 teaspoons fresh garlic, chopped

2 teaspoons fresh ginger, chopped

½ cup white onion, chopped

2 cups portabella mushroom
  (chopped into half-inch pieces)

1 cup celeriac or celery, grated

4 cups Basic Chicken Stock
  (see page 61 for recipe)

1 tablespoon dried parsley

1 teaspoon soy sauce

¼ teaspoon fresh ground black pepper

⅛ teaspoon crushed red pepper flakes

3 tablespoons white sesame seeds

1 cup lacinata kale, chopped
  (may substitute with any variety
  of kale)

◆ In a soup pot heat the olive and sesame oils over medium heat. Add the garlic, ginger and onion, and sauté for 3 to 4 minutes or until onions become transparent.

◆ Add the mushrooms and sauté for 5 minutes.

◆ Add the celeriac and sauté for 5 more minutes.

◆ Add the stock, parsley, soy sauce, black pepper and crushed red pepper. Reduce heat to a simmer and cook until the celeriac is tender, about 45 minutes.

◆ In a small skillet over medium heat, lightly toast the sesame seeds.

◆ Turn off heat and stir the kale into the soup pot. Serve, garnishing each bowl with toasted sesame seeds.

Serves four

HARVEST HINT

Celeriac is the Northeastern version of celery. Celeriac is not an attractive vegetable, but it is a wonderful addition to soup as it functions as a thickening agent. It has a strong celery flavor. Celery can be a challenge to find locally; celeriac is a practical and flavorful substitute, and is available as a storage vegetable all winter long.

ROASTED BUTTERNUT SQUASH
AND APPLE SOUP

1 butternut squash, sliced in half,
  with seeds removed

1 McIntosh apple, peeled,
  cored and cut in half

1 head fresh garlic

1 medium onion, chopped

1 tablespoon olive oil

1 cup apple cider

2 cups vegetable stock

⅛ teaspoon crushed red pepper

Salt and fresh ground black pepper,
  to taste

Garnish

¼ cup non fat sour cream

1 teaspoon pickled jalapeño pepper
  minced (see recipe page 231)

2 tablespoons fresh parsley, chopped

Serves four

◆ Preheat oven to 350 ºF.

◆ Place the squash in a roasting pan, cut side facing up.
Place half of the apple in each center of the squash halves.
Cover and bake for 60 to 75 minutes, or until squash is soft all
the way through. Remove from the oven and let cool slightly.
While the squash is baking, wrap the head of garlic
in aluminum foil (or use a garlic baker if you have one).
Bake for 30 minutes or until soft.

◆ Heat a soup pot over medium heat. Add the onions and
oil and sauté until soft, approximately 10 minutes.

◆ Remove the squash from its skin, and place the squash and
apple in a food processor, including any pan juices. Remove 3
cloves from the baked garlic. Add the 3 garlic cloves and the sautéed onion to the squash, and process until smooth. Add some of
the cider if necessary to blend the squash.

◆ Return the squash mixture to the soup pot. Add the cider,
stock, crushed red pepper, salt and pepper, and simmer for
15 minutes or until heated thoroughly.

◆ In a small bowl mix the jalapeño into the sour cream.
Serve the soup garnished with a dollop of sour cream and jalapeño
mixture, and sprinkle with parsley.

HARVEST HINT

Try to use your oven efficiently by combining foods that require long cooking times. While preparing this recipe, bake an
extra squash to put in the freezer and a head or two of garlic for use in other recipes.

RED CRANBERRY BEAN AND TURKEY SOUP

Meatballs

½ pound ground turkey

1 egg, slightly beaten

¼ cup dry bread crumbs

1 teaspoon dried parsley

1 teaspoon fresh garlic, chopped

⅛ teaspoon fresh ground black pepper

½ teaspoon onion powder

1 tablespoon olive oil

Soup

1 tablespoon olive oil

¾ cup red onion, finely chopped

1 cup carrots, finely chopped

1 tablespoon all-purpose flour

4 cups Basic Chicken Stock
  (see recipe on page 61)

1 cup dried cranberry beans,
  soaked overnight and rinsed

1 teaspoon dried parsley

1 teaspoon dried thyme

⅛ teaspoon fresh ground black pepper

½ cup green shelled peas, frozen

Serves four

◆ To make the meatballs, in a large bowl mix the turkey, egg, bread crumbs, parsley, garlic, pepper and onion powder. Roll into small balls, approximately a half-inch round.

◆ Heat the oil in a large skillet over medium-high heat. Add the meatballs and cook for approximately 12 minutes, gently turning as the meat browns and loosens from the pan. Once lightly browned, remove from heat.

◆ In a soup pot add the second tablespoon of oil. Add the onions and sauté, stirring over medium heat for approximately 5 minutes. Add carrots and continue to cook another 5 minutes. Slowly add the flour to coat the vegetables and cook, stirring, for 2 minutes.

◆ Slowly add the stock, stirring. Add the beans, parsley, thyme and pepper. Bring to a boil for 2 minutes. Reduce heat, cover and simmer for 45 minutes. Add the meatballs and simmer 15 more minutes.

◆ Five minutes before serving add the peas to the soup. Serve.

HARVEST HINT

According to Slow Foods USA, red cranberry beans are one of the oldest American bean varieties, traditionally grown by the Abenaki Indians in Maine. The beans look very much like cranberries, and are a colorful addition to both the garden and the kitchen. Let them dry on the stalk, then shell. Unlike some red beans, these keep their color while cooking. Store them in glass canning jars to show off their beautiful red color.

HEARTY ROOT VEGETABLE CHOWDER

½ cup white onion, chopped

2 tablespoons fresh garlic, chopped

1 tablespoon butter

1 cup rutabaga, peeled and finely
  chopped

1 cup peeled and finely chopped carrot

1 cup peeled and finely
  chopped parsnips

¾ cup white potato, peeled and
  finely chopped

3 cups milk

1 tablespoon dried parsley

½ teaspoon dried thyme

¼ teaspoon salt

¼ teaspoon fresh ground black pepper

⅛ teaspoon crushed red pepper

¼ cup heavy cream

Serves four

◆ Heat a soup pot over medium heat, and add the onion, garlic and butter. Sauté for approximately 5 minutes, or until soft.

◆ Add the rutabaga, carrot, parsnips and potato and cook for 10 minutes, stirring occasionally.

◆ Add the milk, parsley, thyme, salt, black pepper and red pepper. Cover and simmer for 45 minutes.

◆ Add the cream and simmer, uncovered, for an additional 15 minutes. Serve.

HARVEST HINT

Rutabaga is generally harvested in the fall, and is another standard ingredient in a winter farm share because it is a dependable, long-lasting storage vegetable. Rutabaga looks similar to turnip, but is more yellow in color. It is also sweeter than turnip, and milder in flavor. Properly stored rutabaga should be firm and heavy for their size; the skin should be smooth as any wrinkling indicates that it has lost moisture.

• Make a habit of keeping a large tote bag or two in your car so you are always prepared to shop at the market. If you have an extra insulated lunchbox, keep one in the car to store any cheese or meat that you buy, even for a short trip home.

• Shop first at the farmers' market, and then on the way home stop at your local grocery store for those few missing exotic ingredients.

• Don't hesitate to choose the best quality produce, but don't buy too much! Even though so many foods look appetizing, only buy as much as you can eat within four or five days.

Spicy Sesame Beef and Cabbage Soup

1 tablespoon canola oil

1 tablespoon fresh garlic, chopped

1 tablespoon fresh ginger, chopped

½ cup white onion, chopped

1 teaspoon Pickled Jalapeño
   Pepper, minced (see page 231)

1 cup beef, top round or eye of the
   round (or any lean cut of beef),
   cut into strips ¼ x ¼ x 1 inch

1 ½ cups green cabbage, chopped

¾ cups carrots cut into fine strips
   (¹⁄₁₆ x ¹⁄₁₆ x 1 inch)

¾ cup finely chopped rutabaga

4 ½ cups beef stock or Basic Chicken
   Stock (see page 61 for recipe)

¼ cup low-sodium soy sauce

1 tablespoon toasted white
   sesame seeds

¼ cup fresh cilantro, chopped

Serves six

◆ Heat a soup pot over medium-heat. Add oil, garlic, ginger, onions and jalapeño, and sauté for 1 minute.

◆ Add the beef and sauté for 4 minutes, or until beef is just cooked.

◆ Add the cabbage, carrots and rutabaga, and sauté for 1 minute.

◆ Add stock and soy sauce, and bring to a boil. Reduce heat and simmer for 5 minutes.

◆ To toast sesame seeds, heat a small pan over medium heat. Add seeds and toss in pan to prevent burning. Heat for 30 to 60 seconds.

◆ Stir cilantro and sesame seeds into soup pot and simmer for 2 minutes. Serve.

HARVEST HINT

In our winter farm share we get garlic, onion, cabbage, carrots and rutabaga. By adding just a few more exotic ingredients we can transform our local farm bounty into a soup that tastes like it comes from the other side of the world.

BASIC CHICKEN STOCK

Bones of 5 chickens

2 ½ cups onions, roughly chopped

2 cups carrots, roughly chopped

6 stalks celeriac or celery,
  roughly chopped

1 tablespoon black peppercorns

15 sprigs fresh parsley

15 sprigs fresh thyme

4 large fresh garlic cloves

Approximately 6 quarts cold water

Makes seven quarts

◆ In a 12-quart stock pot add the chicken bones and all remaining ingredients.

◆ Cover with enough water to bring within 2 inches from the top of the pot.

◆ Bring to a boil, then reduce heat. Simmer stock for 60 to 90 minutes.

◆ When stock is ready, strain with a fine sieve into a large bowl. Discard bones and vegetables. Refrigerate overnight.

◆ The next day skim off the fat and discard, and pour into quart jars. Stock is ready to use or freeze. Do not fill jars completely if freezing.

HARVEST HINT

Homemade stock is an essential ingredient to keep on hand. Homemade stock is more concentrated in flavor, has a richer color and has a smaller carbon footprint than the store-bought versions. This stock can be frozen for up to six months.

GARDEN GREENS
AND MORE SALADS

In the spring, summer, fall and winter, there are many local ingredients available to create fresh salads. The salad recipes we share are based on what is available from our annual farm shares, at the summer and winter farmers' markets, and what we grow in our own gardens. When writing these recipes, we were challenged by only using what was available and in season. Sometimes we were surprised to find baby greens in December or spinach in the beginning of March, and we also found there to be plenty of cabbage throughout the year. To create salads during the winter season, we chose alternatives to using lettuce in our creations. Some of the foods used were preserved from our summer harvest, as well as root vegetables, apples, cheese, cider and beans. This experience has changed the way we look at making salads in the winter months. These flavorful recipes will satisfy your appetite all year long.

Garden Greens and More Salads

SPRING BLEND

Baby romaine
Arugula
Kale
Baby green leaf
Garlic chives
Chive flowers
Wild Strawberry Ginger Dressing

SUMMER BLEND

Romaine lettuce
Boston bibb
Red leaf lettuce
Dandelion greens
Beet greens
Pansies
Parsley
Buttermilk Chive Dressing

FALL BLEND

Mustard greens
Escarole
Dandelion greens
Nasturtium flowers
Beet greens
Kale
Spinach
Cilantro
Apple Cider Vinaigrette

MIXED GREENS

Creating your own salad mix is easy and you will find a variety of ingredients at your local farmers' market, or you can grow them in your own garden.

There are seasonal greens like arugula, beet, frisée, sorrel, mâche, mesclun, mustard, dandelions and turnip. There are also a variety of lettuces to be found including bibb, green leaf, oak leaf, butterhead and romaine. Make your salads more interesting by including a variety of fresh herbs and edible flowers.

Some of the most popular types of flowers are nasturtiums, chive flowers, pansies and roses; their flavors run from peppery to mild onion to grape, and all are lightly fragrant. For the best nutrition, seek out the dark greens such as spinach, kale, collards and beet greens, and blend with other, lighter greens to give you a tasty mix. Wash your greens and lettuce, but do not soak them in water for more than a minute as they will absorb water and the flavor will wash out. Dry with a lettuce spinner to remove the excess water. We have included a few of our favorite salad mixes and homemade dressing combinations for you to try.

WILD STRAWBERRY GINGER DRESSING

4 tablespoons red wine vinegar

4 tablespoons olive oil

2 tablespoons wild strawberry jam

1 tablespoon shallots, chopped

1 teaspoon fresh ginger, chopped

½ teaspoon fresh garlic, chopped

◆ Using an immersion blender, combine the vinegar, olive oil, jam, shallots, ginger and garlic, and blend the mixture until smooth. This recipe can also be made in a food processor, but the quantities of all ingredients should be doubled.

◆ Dressing can be stored for up to a week in the refrigerator.

HARVEST HINT

Use your homemade strawberry jam in this recipe, or pick one up at your local farmers' market.
For a fresh twist, try using rhubarb-strawberry or raspberry jam.

APPLE CIDER VINAIGRETTE

1½ cups apple cider

5 tablespoons olive oil

1 tablespoon cider vinegar

¼ teaspoon fresh garlic, chopped

½ teaspoon shallots, minced

Pinch of salt

◆ In a small saucepan over medium heat, reduce the cider down to about ¼ cup. It should become slightly thickened, like syrup. Let cool to room temperature.

◆ In a small mixing bowl combine the reduced cider, olive oil, vinegar, garlic, shallots and salt. Whisk together so that all ingredients are well blended.

◆ Vinaigrette can be stored for up to a week in the refrigerator.

HARVEST HINT

If you find yourself with extra cider on hand, reduce it by following the instructions in this recipe, and store in small quantities in the freezer. Reduced cider can be used for dressings, sauces, or can simply be reconstituted.

BUTTERMILK CHIVE DRESSING

¼ cup yogurt

1 tablespoon brown sugar

1 tablespoon cider vinegar

½ cup buttermilk

4 tablespoons fresh chives,
   finely chopped

Pinch salt

Makes ¾ cup

◆ Place the yogurt in a fine sieve and drain for 15 minutes.

◆ Combine the sugar, vinegar, buttermilk, chives and salt in a small bowl, and whisk until blended smoothly.

◆ Add the yogurt and whisk into the dressing. Refrigerate.

◆ Dressing can be stored for up to a week in the refrigerator.

HARVEST HINT

Chives are one of the earliest herbs to come up in the spring, and they last long into the fall. In the spring it can be inspirational to cut the first fresh chives, as it helps us look forward to the other plants that will soon be coming up in the garden and selling in the local markets. The spring blooms are a beautiful purple color and are edible as well. Simply snip the flowers and toss them into your salad to add color. In the fall, chop the chives, lay them out on paper towel in a single layer to dry (takes about one week) and then store in the pantry for winter.

Sweet and Tangy Asian Salad

Dressing

2 teaspoons fresh lemon juice

2 tablespoons olive oil

1 tablespoon maple syrup

2 teaspoons rice wine vinegar

2 teaspoons sesame oil

2 teaspoons fresh garlic, finely chopped

2 tablespoons fresh parsley, chopped

1 tablespoon fresh cilantro, chopped

1 teaspoon fresh ginger, minced

¼ teaspoon fresh ground black pepper

2 tablespoons white sesame seeds

Salad

3 cups Napa cabbage, sliced lengthwise,
   then cut into thin, 2-inch-long strips

1 cup carrot cut matchstick style

2 green onions, sliced lengthwise,
   2-inches long

Serves four

◆ To prepare the dressing, in a small bowl whisk together the lemon juice, olive oil, maple syrup, vinegar, sesame oil, garlic, parsley, cilantro, ginger and pepper. Set aside.

◆ To toast sesame seeds, heat a small pan over medium heat. Add seeds and toss in pan to prevent burning. Heat for 30 to 60 seconds.

◆ In a large bowl combine the cabbage, carrot and green onions and mix thoroughly.

◆ Pour the dressing into the vegetables and toss to coat. Sprinkle with sesame seeds and serve.

HARVEST HINT

Napa cabbage, also called Chinese cabbage, is long with pale green leaves and a white center. It is shaped like a head of romaine lettuce, but is packed very firmly, with crisp leaves. Choose one with crinkled but fresh looking outer leaves and one that is compact and heavy. It is sweeter than green cabbage, and can be a tasty addition to a salad. It can be held in a root cellar for winter storage or stores well in a bag in the refrigerator for five or six days.

RADICCHIO, BROCCOLI AND PEAR SALAD WITH HOMEMADE BLUE CHEESE DRESSING

Salad

2 cups radicchio, chopped (1-inch)

1 ½ cups fresh broccoli, chopped (1-inch)

½ cup fresh pear, chopped

⅛ cup red onion, chopped

1 tablespoon fresh parsley, chopped

½ tablespoon fresh lemon juice

Dressing

2 ounces blue cheese, crumbled

½ cup light sour cream

1 teaspoon fresh garlic, chopped

⅛ teaspoon fresh ground black pepper

Serves four

◆ In a large bowl combine the radicchio, broccoli, pear, onion, parsley and lemon juice; mix thoroughly.

◆ In a food processor, combine the blue cheese, sour cream, garlic and pepper, and process until smooth.

◆ Pour the dressing into the vegetables and toss to coat. Serve.

HARVEST HINT

This is a full-bodied, bold tasting salad and the slight bitterness in the radicchio is offset by the sweet pear taste. Radicchio is Italian in origin, and is recognizable by its red or burgundy leaf color and white stems. When choosing radicchio at the market, avoid heads with brown or yellow spots. Radicchio is quite firm and can even stand up to light grilling, for an unusual side dish.

Vine-Ripened Tomatoes and Cucumber with Lemon Thyme

3 tablespoons olive oil

1 tablespoon balsamic vinegar

1 teaspoon fresh lemon thyme, chopped

1 teaspoon fresh garlic, chopped

1 large tomato, sliced ¼-inch

1 medium cucumber, sliced ¼-inch

⅛ cup red onion, chopped

Fresh ground black pepper

Serves four generously

◆ In a small bowl, whisk together the olive oil, vinegar, thyme and garlic. Set aside.

◆ On a large round plate, lay out the tomatoes and cucumbers, overlapping and alternating the tomatoes and cucumbers.

◆ Sprinkle the red onion over the tomatoes and cucumbers.

◆ Lightly drizzle the olive oil and balsamic vinegar mixture over the tomatoes and cucumbers and around the plate. This salad is best served at room temperature with fresh ground black pepper on top.

HARVEST HINT

This salad can be served as an entrée with the addition of some crumbled goat cheese or feta on top. This recipe can be doubled easily for a larger group.

WHEAT BERRY SALAD WITH
SUMMER VEGETABLES AND GARDEN HERBS

½ cup wheat berries, rinsed

1 tablespoon olive oil

1 cup summer squash, chopped

1 cup zucchini, chopped

½ cup red onion, finely chopped

1 tablespoon garlic, chopped

1 cup fresh tomatoes with juices,
   chopped

¼ cup fresh basil, chopped

2 tablespoons olive oil

2 tablespoons red wine vinegar

2 tablespoons fresh lemon juice

2 tablespoons fresh parsley, chopped

1 tablespoon fresh oregano, chopped

Salt and pepper to taste

Serves four generously

Photo page 62-63

◆ In a large saucepan, add the wheat berries to 4 cups of water. Boil for 2 minutes, reduce heat, cover and simmer for 75 minutes. When cooked, the berries should split open and be chewy in texture. Drain and refrigerate. It is best to cook the berries the day before use.

◆ In a medium saucepan, add the first tablespoon of olive oil and heat over medium heat. Add the squash, zucchini, red onion and garlic, and sauté for approximately 5 minutes or until slightly soft.

◆ Add the squash mixture and tomatoes to the wheat berries, and mix well.

◆ In a small bowl whisk together the basil, remaining 2 tablespoons of oil, vinegar, lemon juice, parsley and oregano. Pour the dressing over the wheat berry mixture, and toss to coat. Add salt and pepper to taste, mix well and serve or refrigerate.

HARVEST HINT

Wheat berries are whole, unprocessed wheat kernels. They have a chewy, firm texture and nutty flavor. They are easy to store and are versatile to keep on hand in the pantry. Cook wheat berries ahead, and store in the refrigerator or freezer to add to soups, salads or to stir up a quick side dish.

WARM RED POTATO SALAD
WITH DILL

1 pound red potatoes

2 hard-boiled eggs, peeled and chopped

⅓ cup green bell pepper,
  finely chopped

½ cup mayonnaise

¼ cup celeriac or celery, chopped

¼ cup red onion, chopped

4 teaspoons red wine vinegar

2 tablespoons fresh dill, chopped

2 teaspoons fresh garlic, chopped

¼ teaspoon salt

¼ teaspoon fresh ground black pepper

Serves eight

◆ Boil the potatoes until tender (when the potatoes can be easily pierced with a knife). Drain the potatoes and cut into half-inch pieces.

◆ In a large bowl combine the potatoes, egg, bell pepper, mayonnaise, celeriac or celery, onion, vinegar, dill, garlic, salt and pepper, and mix well.

◆ Serve or refrigerate.

HARVEST HINT

A healthier variation of this recipe can be made by substituting the egg and mayonnaise with 6 tablespoons of olive oil.

"The things most worth wanting

are not available everywhere,

all the time."

— Alice Waters, from This Organic Life, Joan Gussow

Violetta Insalata

1 eggplant (about 1 pound), sliced into
   long, thin strings (like spaghetti)

2 tablespoons olive oil

⅛ teaspoon sea salt

1 tablespoon fresh lemon juice

1 tablespoon red wine vinegar

1 teaspoon chopped fresh garlic

1 tablespoon fresh basil, chopped

1 tablespoon fresh parsley, chopped

¼ teaspoon fresh ground black pepper

Serves four generously

◆ Bring a large pot of water to a boil.

◆ In the boiling water blanch the eggplant for 30 seconds,
then drain and submerge immediately into cold water with ice.
Drain again.

◆ In a medium bowl, whisk together the oil, salt, lemon juice,
vinegar, garlic, basil, parsley and pepper. Add the eggplant and toss
well. Let rest in the refrigerator for 2 hours to allow the flavors to
meld. Serve with other antipasti foods such as Mushroom Salad.

HARVEST HINT

Olive oil is an essential ingredient in good cooking, although we do consider it to be an exotic ingredient since it is not
available locally in the Northeast. There are good olive oils being produced in California, so depending on where you
live you may actually be able to purchase a local olive oil. Look for other types of oils produced closer to home, such as
safflower or sunflower oils.

CUCUMBER AND SPINACH SALAD
WITH FARM-FRESH FETA

Salad

1 cup cucumber, seeded, chopped

½ cup dried cherries, chopped roughly

1 green onion, chopped

2 ounces feta cheese, cut into
  ¼-inch cubes

6 cups fresh spinach

Dressing

3 tablespoons olive oil

1 tablespoon red wine vinegar

1 tablespoon fresh lemon juice

1 teaspoon dried oregano

⅛ teaspoon fresh ground black pepper

¼ cup pine nuts, toasted

Serves four

◆ In a large bowl, combine the cucumber, cherries, onion, feta and spinach, and mix thoroughly.

◆ To prepare the dressing, in a small bowl whisk together the olive oil, vinegar, lemon juice, oregano and pepper.

◆ To toast pine nuts, heat a small pan over medium heat. Add nuts and toss in pan to prevent burning. Heat for 30 to 60 seconds.

◆ Pour the dressing into the salad mixture and toss lightly to coat. Divide onto serving plates and top with toasted pine nuts. Serve.

HARVEST HINT

Local spinach is planted to harvest in the spring and fall. Large leaf spinach will need to be washed more than once, as it is usually grown in sandy soil and will be gritty. During preparation, remove any large, wood stems. Baby spinach may be a little less work to prepare, but is usually more expensive than the larger leaf spinach.

SLOW COOKED FENNEL AND SHALLOTS OVER MIXED GREENS WITH RASPBERRY DRESSING

Salad

1 medium bulb fennel, sliced ¼-inch
  (should measure about 2 cups)

¾ cup shallots, sliced ¼-inch

1 tablespoon olive oil

2 slices Prosciutto cut into fine strips

4 ounces mixed greens

½ cup fresh raspberries

Dressing

1 cup fresh raspberries (can use frozen
  raspberries that have been thawed)

¼ cup apple cider

4 teaspoons balsamic vinegar

1 tablespoon honey

1 tablespoon ground mustard

Serves four

◆ In a medium saucepan combine the fennel, shallots and olive oil. Heat over low heat for 60 minutes, stirring occasionally. Add a little more olive oil if necessary.

◆ Place the Prosciutto in a small saucepan. Cook over medium heat until crisp. Remove from pan and let cool. Slice the Prosciutto into very thin, small strips. Set aside.

◆ To make the dressing, using a food processor purée the raspberries until very smooth. Strain out the seeds through a fine sieve. In a small bowl combine the strained raspberry purée with cider, vinegar, honey and mustard, and whisk together.

◆ Pour the dressing onto the greens, and toss lightly to coat. Divide the greens onto four plates, and top with the warm fennel mixture. Sprinkle the Prosciutto and fresh raspberries on top, and serve.

HARVEST HINT

Fennel is a vegetable that grows above the ground with a bulb base, celery-like stalks and feathery green leaves.
To prepare fennel, cut the stalks off at the top of the bulb and trim the base. Wash and slice the bulb in half, and slice or dice depending on the recipe. Fennel is becoming more popular so don't hesitate to try it in salads, soups and stews.

Sweet Purple Slaw with Apples and Walnuts

Salad

4 cups red cabbage, sliced
   (¼-inch by 1-inch long)

1 Honeycrisp apple, chopped ¼-inch,
   or 2 cups total

½ small red onion (or ¼ cup), chopped

1 tablespoon lemon juice

½ cup walnuts, chopped

¼ cup dried cranberries

Dressing

⅛ cup red wine vinegar

¼ cup olive oil

⅛ cup maple syrup

⅛ teaspoon salt

⅛ teaspoon fresh ground black pepper

Serves six to eight

◆ In a large bowl mix together the cabbage, apple, onion, lemon juice, walnuts and cranberries.

◆ Prepare the dressing by whisking together the vinegar, olive oil, maple syrup, salt and pepper.

◆ Add the dressing to the cabbage mixture and mix well to coat.

◆ Refrigerate at least 2 hours before serving.

HARVEST HINT

Walnuts are an excellent choice when looking for a plant-based protein to add to a salad. Adding nuts can add interesting texture and good nutrition. Walnuts are the only nut with a significant amount of omega-3 fats, they are low in saturated fat, and contain antioxidants. Black walnut trees grow in cold climate zones so you may be able to find them locally. To keep walnuts fresh, store them in the refrigerator or freezer.

NOTE FROM DIANE

THE HONEYCRISP APPLE

Honeycrisp apples are one of my favorite apple varieties. Every year I visit my local orchard at least once or twice to pick a few bushels.

There are many local orchards close to my home, and all are family-run farms.

Apple picking is a wonderful outing for families in the fall season that helps to connect children to local food. In addition to apple picking, many orchards have other activities for the kids, like hay rides, petting zoos or pony rides which help to make the day memorable.

HARVEST HINT

Apples are available locally beginning in August, and there are large local producers who then store their harvest in a reduced-oxygen environment that preserves the fruit quality for months. This type of storage allows us to eat fresh, crisp, local apple well into winter and even spring.

Roasted Maple Duck with Greens, Squash and Apple Cider Vinaigrette

4 duck legs

Salt

Fresh ground black pepper

½ cup Maple Barbeque Sauce
  (see page 227 for recipe)

1 cup butternut squash,
  finely cut julienne

1 tablespoon olive oil

8 cups mixed baby greens

10 sprigs each of fresh parsley,
  cilantro and dill

½ cup Apple Cider Vinaigrette
  (see page 68 for recipe)

3 tablespoons red onion, finely chopped

Serves four

◆ Preheat the oven to 375 °F. Season the duck legs lightly with salt and pepper. Place in a roasting pan, and roast for about 35 minutes, depending on the size of the duck legs. Cook until the duck reaches an internal temperature of 165 °F. Remove the duck from the oven, and lower the oven temperature to 350 °F.

◆ Drain off any excess fat from the pan. Brush the duck with barbeque sauce, being sure to cover all sides, and return to the oven to roast for another 5 minutes. Repeat.

◆ Remove the duck legs from the oven and set aside until cool enough to handle. Carefully remove the meat from the bone, slice and set aside.

◆ Place the squash in a small bowl, season lightly with salt and pepper and toss in the olive oil. Spread on a small baking pan and cook in the oven for 5 to 10 minutes. This can be done while the duck is roasting. When the squash is just tender remove it from the oven and set aside to cool to room temperature.

◆ In a large bowl place the greens, parsley, cilantro and dill, and add the vinaigrette. Toss to coat the greens evenly. Divide the greens mixture onto large salad plates. Top each plate with an equal portion of duck, top with butternut squash and sprinkle with red onion. You can divide this portion in half to serve as an appetizer for 8 guests.

HARVEST HINT

Avoid covering your salads with heavy dressings made from mayonnaise, which are high in saturated fats and calories. Keep it light and nutritious by drizzling with a high quality olive oil, vinegar and fruit juices. Use just enough to enhance, not mask, the flavor of the fresh food.

"It is only the farmer who faithfully plants seeds in the spring who

reaps a harvest in the autumn".

—Bertie Charles Forbes

SPINACH SALAD WITH
PUMPKIN-SEED-CRUSTED GOAT CHEESE

Salad

1 tablespoon olive oil

½ cup onion, finely chopped

1 teaspoon fresh garlic, finely chopped

⅔ cup pumpkin seeds

6 ounces goat cheese

9 cups fresh spinach, washed

1 carrot, peeled and shaved
  (about 1 cup loosely packed)

Dressing

3 tablespoons olive oil

2 tablespoons balsamic vinegar

1 tablespoon honey

½ tablespoon Dijon-style mustard

Fresh ground black pepper to taste

Serves six

◆ Preheat the oven to 350 ºF.

◆ In a small saucepan heat the olive oil over medium heat. Add the onion and garlic and sauté until slightly browned, approximately 8 minutes. Set aside.

◆ In a food processor, coarsely chop half (⅓ cup) of the pumpkin seeds.

◆ Cut the cheese into 6 wedges or rounds, depending on the shape of the cheese.

◆ Roll the cheese in the chopped pumpkin mixture. Thoroughly coat all sides of the cheese.

◆ Place the cheese on a small baking sheet and bake in the oven for 5 minutes, until the cheese begins to visibly soften. At the same time, on a small baking sheet, bake the remaining ⅓ cup pumpkin seeds until lightly toasted.

◆ To prepare the dressing, in a small bowl whisk together the olive oil, vinegar, honey, mustard and pepper.

◆ In a large bowl toss the spinach with the dressing, the onion and garlic mixture and shaved carrot. Serve on salad plates.

◆ Top each salad with one piece of cheese and the remaining toasted pumpkin seeds.

HARVEST HINT

Pumpkin seeds are now widely available, but it's quite simple to keep it local and make your own. Simply remove the seeds from the pumpkin pulp, and rinse them well. Spread the seeds out on a baking sheet to dry overnight on the counter or in a low temperature oven. When completely dry, remove from the baking sheet and store in a jar. For a quick and healthy snack toss the seeds with olive oil, garlic and salt, and roast in the oven at 350 ºF until lightly browned.

ARUGULA AND PEAR SALAD WITH CHEDDAR AND MAPLE DRESSING

Dressing

½ teaspoon garlic, minced

¼ cup olive oil

2 tablespoons balsamic vinegar

1 tablespoon maple syrup

Salad

4 cups arugula, washed, stems removed
  and dried

1 red pear, sliced about ¼-inch

4 thin slices red onion

¼ cup pecan halves

2 ounces sharp cheddar cheese,
  diced small or cut into fine strips
  for garnish

Serves four

◆ Using an immersion blender, combine the garlic, olive oil, vinegar and maple syrup, and blend the mixture until smooth.

◆ Place the arugula in a large bowl and add the pear, onion and pecans.

◆ Add the dressing to the salad and toss to coat. Garnish with cheddar cheese and serve.

HARVEST HINT

Arugula is a bright green, tender leafy green that looks similar to an oak leaf in shape. Arugula leaves are crisp but delicate, and have stringy stems which should be cut away during preparation. The young leaves are pungent in flavor and the older leaves are larger, darker and more tart. Both complement the sweetness of fresh fruit when served in a salad like this.

Kale and Fennel Salad with Apples and Cinnamon

Dressing

3 tablespoons olive oil

2 tablespoons honey

2 tablespoons cider vinegar

1 teaspoon fresh garlic, chopped

¼ tsp ground cinnamon

Salad

½ cup fennel, julienne (⅛ -inch by
 ⅛-inch by 2-inch)

½ cup apple, julienne
 (use Honeycrisp, Empire
 or Red Delicious)

½ cup carrots, julienne

¼ cup red onion, julienne

1 cup kale, finely chopped

Serves four

◆ Using an immersion blender or whisk, combine the olive oil, honey, vinegar, garlic and cinnamon, and blend until smooth.

◆ In a large bowl combine the fennel, apple, carrot and onion.

◆ Add the dressing to the vegetables and mix well. There will be more dressing than needed and the salad will appear slightly wet.

◆ Evenly divide the chopped kale onto salad plates. Evenly divide the salad mixture on top of the kale; the extra dressing will coat the kale. Serve.

HARVEST HINT

Kale is a member of the cabbage family, and has a reputation for being strong flavored and tougher than most greens, but its sturdy leaves allow it to hold up to cooking better than other greens. Kale is available well into the winter months, and in fact, freezing makes kale sweeter. There are many varieties of kale and all can be used in the same way, so don't hesitate to use whatever variety is available in any recipe that calls for kale (or even as a substitute for spinach). Kale is packed with nutrients; to maintain the most nutrition cook kale leaves briefly, until just crisp-tender.

ROASTED TWO BEET SALAD

½ cup red wine vinegar

¼ cup olive oil

1 tablespoon maple syrup
   (can use honey as a substitute)

1 teaspoon fresh garlic, minced

1 teaspoon fresh lemon thyme, minced

1 teaspoon salt

4 medium beets, roasted, peeled and
   cut julienne (use both red and
   golden beets)

½ cup red onion, sliced

Serves four

◆ Prepare the dressing by whisking together the vinegar, olive oil, maple syrup, garlic, thyme and salt.

◆ In a small bowl combine the beets and onions, and pour in the dressing. Mix well.

◆ Refrigerate for 60 minutes and serve.

HARVEST HINT

To roast beets, wash and lightly coat with olive oil. Sprinkle with salt and pepper, place in a preheated oven and roast at 375 °F for 45 to 60 minutes. Test for tenderness by piercing with a sharp knife; there will be no resistance when they are ready. Place beets in a bowl and cover. When they are cool enough to handle, the skin should rub off easily, and don't forget to remove the woody ends. If you are concerned about stained hands, wear food-safe gloves!

GRILLED MAINE SHRIMP WITH
WARM CANNELLINI BEAN SALAD

Salad

2 cups cooked cannellini beans

1 tablespoon onion, finely chopped

2 tablespoons olive oil

2 teaspoons red wine vinegar

1 tablespoon fresh basil, chopped

1 tablespoon fresh parsley, chopped

1 tablespoon fresh lemon juice

½ tablespoon fresh garlic, chopped

¼ teaspoon crushed red pepper

⅛ teaspoon salt

⅛ teaspoon fresh ground black pepper

Shrimp

¾ pound (approximately 12) fresh
 Maine shrimp, peeled and deveined

1 tablespoon olive oil

1 tablespoon fresh lemon juice

2 tablespoons red bell pepper, chopped,
 for garnish (optional)

Serves four

◆ In a medium sauté pan, add the beans, onion, olive oil, vinegar, basil, parsley, lemon juice, garlic, crushed red pepper, salt and pepper. Over medium heat, sauté for approximately three minutes or until flavors are well blended. Do not overcook or the beans may become mushy.

◆ Toss the shrimp with the olive oil and grill the shrimp over medium heat for 3 minutes, or until completely pink. If cooking on the stovetop, cook in a medium sauté pan over medium heat for 3 minutes, or until completely pink. Drizzle shrimp with lemon juice.

◆ Divide the warm bean mixture onto serving plates, and top with the grilled shrimp. Garnish each plate with the chopped red bell pepper. Serve.

HARVEST HINT

Locally grown dried beans are slowly becoming easier to find. Look for them beginning in late September in farmers' markets and in local grocery stores throughout the winter. If you are able to buy directly from a farmer, some will sell dried beans at a lower price if you are willing to do some of the work and shell them yourself. If you have a winter farm share, you may be pleasantly surprised to find a few pounds of beans included.

Winter Kohlrabi and Cherry Salad

Dressing

1 tablespoon black currant vinegar

1 ½ tablespoons olive oil

1 teaspoon fresh garlic, minced

1 teaspoon honey

1 teaspoon dried parsley

1 teaspoon dried crushed oregano

⅛ teaspoon fresh ground black pepper

Dash salt

Salad

2 cups kohlrabi (any color), thinly sliced

1 cup celeriac or celery, peeled
  and thinly sliced

½ teaspoon fresh lemon juice

⅓ cup dried cherries

⅛ cup white onion, minced

Serves four

◆ Prepare the dressing by whisking together the vinegar, olive oil, garlic, honey, parsley, oregano, pepper and salt.

◆ In a large bowl mix the kohlrabi, celeriac or celery, lemon juice, dried cherries and onion.

◆ Add the dressing to the vegetables and mix well. Serve.

HARVEST HINT

If you are a gardener there is no time like the month of January to plan ahead for a year of harvest. The seed catalogs usually arrive just after the holidays, and the dark nights of January leave time for daydreaming about seeds and plants, and where they might fit in your garden or yard. January is also a great time to organize a seed swap. Invite over fellow gardeners, with instructions to bring a warm dish and some of their favorite seeds to share.

MARKET MEATS, POULTRY AND LOTS OF OTHER ENTRÉES

The production of meat can have a large carbon footprint, so we encourage you to choose your meats carefully, focus on smaller portion sizes and eat plant-based proteins more often.

You will find many meat, fish and poultry recipes as well as vegetarian entrées that include harvest hints written to encourage you to think differently about how and where you buy these foods, and to be conscious of how the animals have been raised. We also include hints for substituting ingredients to help you prepare these entrée recipes in different seasons.

Market Meats, Poultry and Lots of Other Entrées

Spring Steelhead Trout with Sorrel Pesto

1 ½ pounds steelhead trout

Salt to season

3 cups fresh sorrel

6 garlic scapes (if necessary substitute
  with 3 tablespoons fresh garlic,
  chopped)

⅓ cup olive oil

3 tablespoons fresh lemon juice

½ teaspoon fresh ground black pepper

Serves four

◆ Preheat oven to 375 ºF.

◆ Lightly salt the trout and place in a ceramic casserole dish.

◆ Place the sorrel, garlic scapes, olive oil, lemon juice and pepper in a food processor, and process until mixed but still slightly chunky.

◆ Evenly coat the trout with the sorrel pesto. Place in the oven and cook for approximately 25 minutes, or until flesh is firm and flaky.

◆ Remove from the oven, cut into four portions and serve.

HARVEST HINT

Steelhead trout are migratory, lake-run rainbow trout, and run in the coldest streams of Vermont in April. If you are not a fisherman yourself, you may be lucky enough to know someone who enjoys early spring fishing and who is willing to share their catch with you.

OVEN BRAISED CHICKEN WITH WINE, MUSHROOMS AND ONIONS

4 chicken legs, including thigh

½ cup all-purpose flour

2 teaspoons olive oil

16 medium mushrooms,

   cut into quarters

12 small white boiling onions, peeled

   (boiling onions are about one-inch

   in diameter)

2 teaspoons fresh garlic, chopped

2 cups white wine

1 cup Basic Chicken Stock

   (see recipe on page 61)

2 teaspoons fresh parsley, chopped

1 teaspoon fresh rosemary,

   finely chopped

½ teaspoon fresh ground black pepper

1 teaspoon salt

Water

Fresh parsley, chopped, for garnish

Serves four

◆ Preheat the oven to 375 ºF.

◆ Dredge the chicken in the flour and set aside. Reserve the extra flour in a small bowl for use later in the recipe.

◆ Heat a baking skillet or an oval roaster over medium heat. Add the olive oil and the chicken, and sear on each side until golden brown (about 4 minutes on each side). Remove the chicken from heat and set aside.

◆ Add the mushrooms, onions and garlic to the pan, and sauté for 1 minute. Add the wine and stock and deglaze the pan. Add the parsley, rosemary and pepper, and mix. Return chicken to the pan.

◆ Place the pan in the 375 ºF oven, and bake until chicken reaches an internal temperature of 165 ºF, about 35 to 40 minutes. Remove from the oven and place pan on the stove top. Remove the chicken, cover and set aside. Bring the liquids in the pan to a boil and add salt.

◆ Add 3 tablespoons of water to the remaining flour and mix until smooth. Whisk half of this flour mixture into the pan and cook to thicken. If necessary, add more of the flour mixture to thicken the sauce. When sauce is thickened return the chicken to the pan and turn off heat.

◆ To serve, arrange chicken on plates and ladle sauce on top. Garnish with chopped parsley.

Oven Poached Salmon with
Fresh Garden Herbs

15 white onions, julienne strips

10 fresh carrots, julienne strips

10 celery, julienne strips

4 six-ounce salmon fillets,
  skinned and de-boned

1 cup Chardonnay wine

4 lemon slices, ¼-inch thick

6 sprigs fresh thyme
  (lemon thyme if available)

6 sprigs fresh rosemary

6 sprigs fresh parsley

¼ teaspoon cracked black peppercorns

Serves four

◆ Preheat the oven to 350 °F.

◆ In a ceramic casserole dish large enough to fit all of the fillets, spread out the onions, carrots and celery on the bottom.

◆ Arrange the salmon fillets on top of the vegetables.

◆ Pour the wine over the salmon, and place a slice of lemon on each fish fillet. Place the sprigs of herbs and peppercorns on top of the salmon. Cover.

◆ Bake for 20 to 25 minutes or until fish is firm and flaky. Serve.

HARVEST HINT

This recipe is a good example of how to transition your cooking between seasons. In early spring there are not many fresh vegetables available locally, so use the last of your stored carrots and onions, as we do in this recipe. We think that it is reasonable to supplement the local food supply occasionally with vegetables grown elsewhere; in this recipe we use celery which would not be available at this time of year. The herbs used here might be wintered inside or plants bought at this time of year intended for planting in the spring garden.

An overcrowded chicken farm produces fewer eggs.

— A Chinese proverb

Grilled Habanero Chicken with Fresh Cherry Chutney

Fresh Cherry Chutney

1 cup fresh cherries,
  cut in half and pitted

¼ cup green onions, chopped

1 tablespoon cider vinegar

1 tablespoon fresh cilantro, chopped

Habanero Chicken

2 tablespoons FolkFoods
  Master Sauce

2 tablespoons olive oil

1 teaspoon honey

4 chicken breasts, boneless
  and skinless

Serves four

◆ In a small bowl, combine the cherries, green onions, cider vinegar and cilantro. Mix well and set aside.

◆ In a large mixing bowl, add the Master Sauce, olive oil and honey, and mix together using a whisk. Add the chicken breasts and toss to coat.

◆ Preheat grill to medium heat. Place the chicken on grill and cook for 10 to 15 minutes, or until it reaches an internal temperature of 165 °F. Arrange on plates and top each with the cherry chutney.

IN COMMERCIAL POULTRY OPERATIONS arsenical compounds are routinely added to feed. If you buy your poultry direct from the farm, specifically ask your farmer about feed additives. You can also be informed when buying poultry in the supermarket by looking for the following labels, which indicate that no arsenical compounds have been used: USDA Organic, Certified Humane or Food Alliance Certified.

HARVEST HINT

Later in the summer when fresh plums are plentiful they can be substituted for the cherries in this chutney recipe. The honey mellows the heat in this recipe, so if you like your food really hot and spicy, add another tablespoon of Master Sauce to the marinade. Master Sauce is made in Vermont by FolkFoods (www.folkfoods.com).

TO ASSURE THAT YOU ARE PURCHASING FISH that is the most healthful and sustainable, we recommend using the pocket-sized guide that can be found on the Monterey Bay Aquarium website. It includes regional lists of fish and seafood that are ranked by best choice, good alternatives and those to avoid. The ranking is based on management and abundance of the species, and the environmental impact of the fishing or farming methods.

OATMEAL-CRUSTED TROUT
WITH PECANS AND LEEKS

4 trout fillets (about 5 to 6 ounces each)

½ cup milk

1 cup rolled oats

½ teaspoon fresh rosemary

½ teaspoon fresh thyme

2 teaspoons lemon peel, grated

¼ teaspoon fresh ground black pepper

Pinch of salt

2 tablespoons canola oil

2 tablespoons butter

1 cup leeks, washed and chopped

½ cup unsalted pecans

1 fresh lemon, juiced

Serves four

◆ Rinse the trout fillets under cold water, place in bowl with milk and set aside for 15 minutes.

◆ Combine rolled oats, rosemary and thyme in an herb grinder or food processor, and process until a flour forms.

◆ Place this oat flour mixture in a bowl. Add lemon peel, pepper and salt, and sift together with a fork until mixed well.

◆ Heat oil in a large sauté pan over medium heat.

◆ Remove the trout from the milk and place in the oat flour mixture to coat. Place in sauté pan, flesh side down. Cook for about 5 minutes until fish is golden brown. Turn trout and sauté for another 2 minutes. Remove trout and arrange on warm serving platter. Repeat with the remaining fillets.

◆ Heat butter in the pan over high heat. Add leeks and cook quickly for 1 to 2 minutes, until leeks are just tender. Add pecans and lemon juice, and sauté for 1 minute. Spoon leeks and pecans over trout and serve.

HARVEST HINT

Rolled oats are much more than just a hot breakfast cereal. Rolled oats are nutritious and high in fiber, so use them often by adding them to other cold cereals, baked goods, stuffing or burgers. Locally harvested oats are now more likely to be available in your neighborhood natural foods store or market; if you see them on the shelves in the fall, stock up as sometimes the supply is limited.

Butterflied Pork Tenderloin with Maple Blackberry Barbeque Sauce

2 pork tenderloins, weighing
  1 ¾ to 2 pounds total
⅓ cup grilling rub (recipe below)
1 cup Maple Blackberry Barbeque Sauce
  (see page 227 for recipe)

Serves six

◆ Place the first tenderloin on a cutting board. Trim most of the visible fat. Butterfly the tenderloin by slicing it length-wise about three quarters of the way through. Lay the sides down to open it up (see photos 1 and 2). Next, slice each side three quarters of the way through (see photo 3). Lay both sides out flat (see photo 4).

◆ Cover pork with plastic wrap and, using a meat mallet, gently pound the tenderloin until it is about a half-inch thick (see photo 5). Remove plastic. Repeat these steps using the second tenderloin.

◆ Rub both sides of the pork with the grilling rub (see photo 6). Cover and let marinate for 1 to 2 hours in the refrigerator.

◆ Preheat the grill to medium-high. Place the pork on the grill for about 10 minutes. Turn over and grill for another 5 minutes.

◆ Brush the barbeque sauce onto the pork and continue to cook for another 4 minutes, turning pork and brushing on more barbeque sauce. Repeat every 3 to 4 minutes until the sauce is finished. Remove from grill and slice in half lengthwise and then into one inch strips. Stack on plates to serve.

Grilling Rub Ingredients

¼ cup chili powder

¼ cup paprika

¼ cup garlic powder

¼ cup onion powder

¼ cup maple sugar

1 ½ teaspoons salt

1 ½ teaspoons fresh ground
  black pepper

Grilling Rub Instructions

◆ In a small jar combine the chili powder, paprika, garlic powder, onion powder, maple sugar, salt and pepper, and shake to mix. Use the rub for the pork tenderloin, and save the remainder for use on other grilled foods, such as chicken or beef.

Butterflying Pork Tenderloin
—A How-To

The art of butterflying pork tenderloin is truly that—*an art*. See recipe instructions on page 104, in the first three paragraphs.

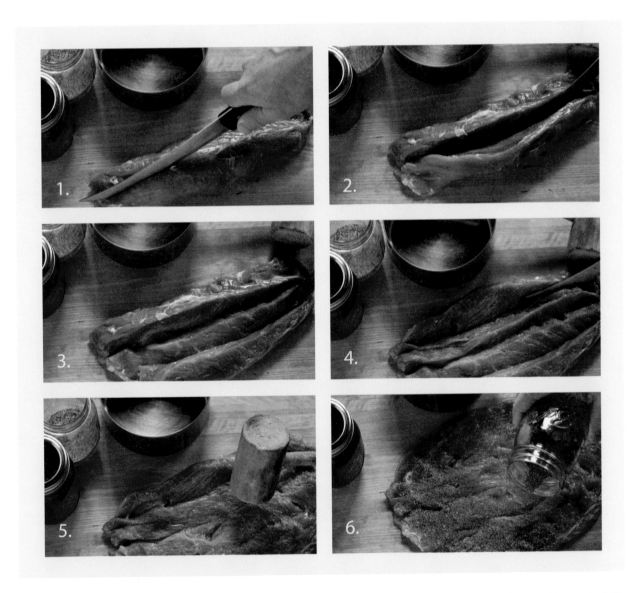

GRILLED MEDITERRANEAN FLANK STEAK WITH FRESH PEAR CHUTNEY

For the Grilling Rub

1 tablespoon plus 1 teaspoon
   ground cumin

1 teaspoon dried mustard

1 teaspoon nutmeg

2 teaspoons brown sugar

2 teaspoons fresh ground black pepper

1 teaspoon kosher salt

1 teaspoon garlic powder

For the Steak

1 flank steak weighing about 1½ pounds

1 recipe of Fresh Pear Chutney

Serves four

◆ Measure all ingredients for the rub and place in a small bowl. Mix well.

◆ Rub both sides of the steak with the grilling rub. Cover and marinate for 2 to 4 hours in the refrigerator.

◆ Preheat the grill to medium-high. Place the steak on the grill and cook to the desired doneness. Serve with Fresh Pear Chutney.

FRESH PEAR CHUTNEY

¾ cup small pears, chopped	¼ teaspoon fresh garlic, chopped
2 tablespoons honey	1 tablespoon red onion, chopped
2 tablespoons cider	1 tablespoon cider vinegar
¼ teaspoon fresh ginger root, chopped	¼ teaspoon jalapeño pepper, chopped

◆ In a small skillet combine the pears, honey, cider, ginger, garlic, onion, vinegar and jalapeño pepper.
◆ Bring quickly to a boil and then reduce the heat to a simmer. Cook for about 5 to 8 minutes until almost all liquid has evaporated.
◆ Remove from heat and refrigerate. To preserve Fresh Pear Chutney for another season, place the hot chutney in sterilized jars, seal and process in a hot water bath for 15 minutes.

HARVEST HINT

Fresh pears should be picked when still firm, as they ripen after picking. Consider using pears in place of apples in many of your favorite homemade preserve recipes, such as pear sauce, butter or nectar, or combine pears with other fruits in jams, jellies and conserves.

GRILLED LAMB BURGERS WITH FRESH KIWI AND CUCUMBER SALSA AND FOCACCIA

1 pound fresh ground lamb

⅓ cup white onion, chopped

1 egg, slightly beaten

¼ cup homemade dried
  whole-wheat bread crumbs

1½ teaspoons Dijon-style mustard

1 tablespoon fresh parsley, chopped

1 tablespoon fresh cilantro, chopped

¼ teaspoon dried crushed oregano

⅛ teaspoon fresh ground black pepper

Fresh Kiwi and Cucumber Salsa
  (see page 110 for recipe)

Focaccia (see page 155 for recipe)

Serves four

◆ In a large bowl mix together the lamb, onion, egg, bread crumbs, mustard, parsley, cilantro, oregano and pepper. Form into 4 patties. These can be made ahead, covered and refrigerated.

◆ Preheat the grill on high. Place the patties on the grill, reduce the heat to medium and cook for approximately 10 minutes, turning once. Internal temperature of the patties should reach 155 °F when fully cooked.

◆ Serve on a toasted Focaccia, topped with Fresh Kiwi and Cucumber Salsa.

HARVEST HINT

Local grass-fed lamb is much milder in flavor than imported lamb, which is often flown in from other countries. When purchasing a whole lamb, we recommend that you buy from a reputable farmer—visit the farm if you have the opportunity, and check that they use a USDA inspected slaughterhouse. When you buy a lamb share you will have your choice of cuts and how you would like them packaged, so select the package sizes that best suit your family.

FRESH KIWI AND CUCUMBER SALSA

1 ½ cups kiwi, chopped

1 cucumber, peeled, seeded and
   chopped (1 ⅓ cups)

1 cup red bell pepper, chopped

¼ cup red onion, chopped

2 tablespoons fresh cilantro, chopped

1 tablespoon fresh mint, chopped

2 teaspoons fresh garlic, minced

1 teaspoon fresh jalapeño pepper,
   minced

1 teaspoon red wine vinegar

1 teaspoon olive oil

Makes approximately
3 ½ cups of salsa

◆ In a large bowl combine the kiwi, cucumber, bell pepper, onion, cilantro, mint, garlic, jalapeño, vinegar and olive oil. Mix well and refrigerate for 2 hours before serving.

◆ Serve with lamb burgers. This recipe will make more salsa than you need for lamb burgers, but it also goes well served with Chipotle Tortilla Chips (see recipe page 27).

HARVEST HINT

At first, kiwi may not seem to be a local food, but there is a hardy variety that grows in the Northeast. Hardy kiwis are quite easily grown, produce smooth-skinned fruit and are a productive addition to any garden. The fruit is ready for harvest in the early fall, and each kiwi vine can harvest between 50 to 100 pounds of fruit. There is no need to peel the fruit before eating, and there will be plenty of fruit to preserve and share with your neighbors.

PAN-SEARED DUCK BREAST
WITH CRANBERRIES

4 duck breasts, 7 to 8 ounces each

¼ teaspoon kosher salt

¼ teaspoon fresh ground black pepper

2 oranges, juiced

2 cups Basic Chicken Stock
 (see page 61 for recipe)

½ cup red wine

2 tablespoons orange peel, finely grated

2 tablespoons maple sugar

⅔ cup fresh or frozen cranberries

Serves four

◆ Preheat the oven to 350 °F.

◆ Rub the duck with the salt and pepper.

◆ Using an oval roaster or a sauté pan that will fit in your oven, heat over medium-high and place the duck breast in the pan, skin side down. Cook until the skin is nicely browned.

◆ Transfer the pan to the oven and bake for 30 to 40 minutes or until cooked (when duck reaches 130 to 135 °F for medium doneness).

◆ In a medium saucepan, add the orange juice, stock, wine, orange peel and maple sugar. Heat over medium until the liquid is reduced by half.

◆ Remove the duck from the pan, cover and keep warm. Remove excess fat from the pan. Add the reduced liquid and cranberries to the pan and cook on the stove over medium heat, until the sauce is reduced to a dark glaze. Pour over the duck breasts and serve.

HARVEST HINT

Cranberries are a perfect winter storage fruit. When they are available locally, stock up and store for up to two months in the refrigerator, or freeze or dry them for later use. Before you store, remove any blemished or dried up fruit from the rest. Cranberries are a great local source of vitamin C and other antioxidants.

COQ AU VIN WITH ROASTED LEEKS

1 whole chicken, approximately

   4 ½ pounds

½ teaspoon fresh rosemary

1 teaspoon garlic, finely chopped

1 teaspoon olive oil

¼ teaspoon salt

¼ teaspoon fresh ground black pepper

2 leeks

1 tablespoon all-purpose flour

½ cup red wine

¾ cup Basic Chicken Stock

   (see page 61 for recipe)

Fresh ground black pepper, to season

Salt, to season

Serves four

◆ Preheat oven to 375 °F.

◆ Remove any excess fat and giblet bag, then rinse the inside and outside of the chicken and pat dry.

◆ Mix together the rosemary, garlic, olive oil, salt and pepper to form a light paste. Rub the outside of the chicken with this paste, to coat.

◆ Place the chicken in a roasting pan. Put in the oven and roast for 20 minutes. Reduce the heat to 350 °F, and continue to roast for 40 minutes or until the chicken reaches an internal temperature of 165 °F.

◆ While the chicken is roasting, wash and cut the leeks (white sections only) into ¼-inch by 2-inch strips.

◆ When the chicken is cooked, remove it from the pan, cover and set aside. Drain off all juices and reserve.

◆ Add the leeks to the roasting pan and cook, stirring for 10 minutes or until leeks are wilted but still bright green. Remove the leeks from the pan and set aside.

◆ Place the roasting pan on the stovetop. Turn the heat to medium, and add the flour and 1 tablespoon of reserved pan drippings. Stir together and cook for 2 to 3 minutes until flour turns light brown.

◆ Add the red wine and chicken stock and whisk to blend in the flour. Bring to a boil, reduce heat to a fast simmer and reduce until the liquid becomes of sauce consistency. Add salt and pepper to taste. Place in a small serving bowl.

◆ Arrange the leeks in the center of a serving platter. Cut the chicken from the bones and place on top of the leeks. Serve with sauce on the side.

ROASTED LAMB WITH GARLIC AND MINT

5 pound boneless leg of lamb

6 full mint stems with leaves

10 cloves fresh garlic, peeled

¼ cup fresh mint leaves

2 tablespoons olive oil

Fresh ground black pepper

Serves ten

◆ Preheat oven to 450 °F.

◆ Cut the excess fat from the lamb leg, if necessary.

◆ In the cut where the bone was removed, layer the whole mint leaves (including stems) and garlic along the middle of the leg.

◆ Using kitchen string, tie the leg closed.

◆ Crush the remaining mint leaves in a mortar or grind in an herb grinder. Add the olive oil, mix and brush onto the outside of the lamb. Generously pepper the outside of the lamb and place in a roasting pan.

◆ Roast for 15 minutes at 450 °F and then reduce the oven temperature to 350 °F. Continue to cook for another 90 minutes, or until the internal temperature reaches 145 °F. Cover and let stand for 15 minutes.

◆ Slice on the diagonal and serve.

HARVEST HINT

Lamb is meat that is produced from sheep that are less than one year old, and spring lamb is from sheep that are harvested between March and October. Although lamb is available commercially year round, this may not always be the case with a smaller, local farm. The most economical way to buy meat is to buy a whole animal directly from the farmer. If a whole lamb, cow or pig is too much meat, plan to split it with another family. Not only does this benefit you in terms of dollars saved on your grocery bill, it helps the farmer economically since he receives the full payment directly.

GINGER BLACK BEAN AND PUMPKIN CAKES WITH CREAMY HORSERADISH

Creamy Horseradish

¼ cup nonfat sour cream

2 tablespoons fresh cilantro, chopped

1 teaspoon fresh lime juice

½ teaspoon Homegrown Horseradish
  (see page 229 for recipe)

¼ teaspoon fresh garlic, chopped

Cakes

1 cup black beans, cooked and
  lightly mashed

½ cup fresh pumpkin, peeled
  and shredded

1 egg, slightly beaten

1 green onion, chopped
  (about 2 tablespoons)

¼ cup dried homemade bread crumbs

2 tablespoons fresh cilantro, chopped

1 tablespoon fresh ginger, chopped

1 tablespoon fresh parsley, chopped

1 teaspoon fresh garlic, chopped

1 teaspoon fresh lime juice

⅛ teaspoon cayenne pepper

Olive oil to sauté

Serves four

◆ In a small bowl mix together the sour cream, cilantro, lime juice, horseradish and garlic. Set aside.

◆ To make the cakes, in a medium bowl mix together the black beans, pumpkin, egg, green onion, bread crumbs, cilantro, ginger, parsley, garlic, lime juice and cayenne pepper. Form into 8 patties.

◆ In a large sauté pan, add enough olive oil to lightly cover the bottom. Heat the oil over medium, add patties and cook 5 minutes on each side. Serve 2 cakes each, with a dollop of the Creamy Horseradish on top.

HARVEST HINT

To prepare dried beans follow these steps:
• Spread beans out on a cloth and pick out any small pieces of dirt or stones.
• Rinse the beans in cool water.
• Place the beans in a bowl or pot and cover with three times the volume of water.
• Soak the beans for up to eight hours at room temperature or slightly longer in the refrigerator.
• Cooking time for beans will depend on the type of bean and the recipe. To cook beans, bring them to a boil, then reduce and simmer until beans are tender but still firmly hold their shape.

Beer-Braised Lamb Shanks with Fennel

2 teaspoons dried fennel seed

2 teaspoons dried oregano, chopped

⅛ teaspoon salt

¼ teaspoon fresh ground black pepper

1 ¾ to 2 pounds lamb shank

1 tablespoon olive oil

1 tablespoon butter

⅓ cup shallots, chopped

2 tablespoons fresh garlic, chopped

1 bottle beer (medium amber)

2 carrots, cut in half

1 medium-size fennel bulb,

  cut in quarters

Serves four

◆ Preheat oven to 350 °F.

◆ On a plate mix together the fennel seed, oregano, salt and pepper. Coat the lamb shanks in the seasoning mixture.

◆ Add the olive oil and butter to a searing pan over medium- to medium-high heat. Add the lamb shanks and sear on all sides until they are evenly browned. Set aside.

◆ To the searing pan add the shallots and garlic. Cook for 1 minute. Add half of the beer to the pan. Return the lamb back to the pan, cover and cook for 60 minutes.

◆ Add the remaining beer to the pan, and turn the lamb. Cook for 40 minutes. Add the carrots and fennel and cook for 25 minutes. Remove the pan from the oven; lamb should be very tender and come off the bone easily. Serve the shank on a platter with the vegetables and pan gravy.

HARVEST HINT

Lamb shanks will be included when you buy a whole lamb share, but many people are not familiar with this cut. Shanks are less tender than some of the other, more expensive cuts, but are just as tasty. Slow, moist cooking in this recipe results in a tender, richly flavored meal.

GRILLED HONEY BOURBON PORK CHOPS
WITH CILANTRO APPLES

Marinade

2 tablespoons honey

2 tablespoons bourbon

1 teaspoon fresh garlic, finely chopped

2 tablespoons onion, minced

3 tablespoons soy sauce

¼ teaspoon fresh ground black pepper

1 teaspoon red wine vinegar

4 center cut pork chops

1 large apple, julienne

1 tablespoon fresh cilantro, chopped

Serves four

◆ In a small bowl combine the honey, bourbon, garlic, onion, soy sauce, pepper and vinegar, and mix well.

◆ Place pork in a shallow pan and pour the marinade over the chops, turning to cover both sides. Marinate the pork chops in the refrigerator for 3 hours, turning over to coat with marinade three times.

◆ Preheat the grill to medium. Grill pork chops on grill for 15 to 20 minutes, turning often so the chops do not burn. Cook until the chops reach an internal temperature of at least 145 °F.

◆ In a small bowl mix together the apple and cilantro. Serve pork over apple cilantro mixture.

HARVEST HINT

Honey has been harvested for over 9000 years, and is now a staple in almost every farmers' market across the country. There are over 300 varieties produced in the United States, ranging in color from pale golden to dark amber and representing unique flavors based on the flora found regionally. In addition to bottled honey, you can purchase honey in its natural state by buying honeycomb, which is entirely edible. Honey should not be stored in the refrigerator as it will crystallize and become cloudy; if this happens it can be clarified by briefly heating the honey.

GRASS-FED BEEF

For centuries we ate pasture-raised beef, but things changed around the middle of the last century when we moved to a more industrialized system of agriculture.

Now it's back to the farm, and the discovery that pasture-raised beef is a healthier product when compared to conventional beef.

Beef from grass-fed cows has a fat ratio that is better for us, with higher omega-3 fats and conjugated linoleic acids (or CLAs).

Enjoy it in moderation, since it is high on the food chain, and thus has a larger carbon footprint.

Rib-Eye Steak with Jalapeño Marinade and Roasted Tomatillos

For the marinade

3 tablespoons fresh lime juice

1 tablespoon olive oil

1 tablespoon honey

1 tablespoon fresh garlic, chopped

1 tablespoon fresh jalapeño pepper, chopped

1 tablespoon cilantro, chopped

¾ teaspoon chili powder

½ teaspoon soy sauce

1 ½ pounds rib-eye (one each per person, or half each if very large)

For the tomatillo sauce

16 medium-sized tomatillos, peeled

1 tablespoon olive oil

1 tablespoon fresh garlic, chopped

1 tablespoon white onion, chopped

Pinch of fresh ground black pepper

Serves four

◆ In a small bowl, combine the lime juice, olive oil, honey, garlic, jalapeño, cilantro, chili powder and soy sauce. Stir well.

◆ Lay out the rib-eye in a pan so that they do not overlap. Pour the marinade over the rib-eye, and turn to coat. Marinate in the refrigerator for at least 2 hours, turning at least once.

◆ Preheat the oven to 350 °F.

◆ In a small roasting pan, combine the tomatillos, tablespoon of olive oil, fresh garlic, onion and black pepper. Stir to coat with oil. Roast in the oven 60 minutes.

◆ Preheat the grill to medium-high heat. Place the steak on the grill and cook to the desired doneness. Divide the tomatillo sauce onto 4 plates, and serve the rib-eye on top of the sauce.

PORK TENDERLOIN STUFFED WITH APPLES AND CHESTNUTS

¼ cup onion, chopped

2 teaspoons olive oil

1 small McIntosh apple, chopped
(about 1 cup)

4 whole chestnuts, shelled and chopped

¼ teaspoon dried parsley, chopped

Pinch fresh ground black pepper

1 large pork tenderloin

1 teaspoon olive oil

⅓ cup Basic Chicken Stock
(see page 61 for recipe)

⅓ cup port

Serves four

◆ Preheat the oven to 350 °F.

◆ Heat the olive oil in a large sauté pan over medium heat. Add the onion and cook for approximately 5 minutes, or until the onions soften. Add the apples, chestnuts, parsley and pepper, and sauté for another 5 minutes.

◆ Slice the tenderloin lengthwise three-quarters of the way through, being careful not to slice all the way through. Stuff the pork with the apple mixture. Using kitchen string, tie the pork closed.

◆ Using the same pan as above, heat the remaining olive oil over medium-high heat, and add the pork. Quickly brown all sides. Transfer the pork to a roasting pan and cook in the oven for approximately 20 minutes, or until an internal temperature of 145 °F is reached.

◆ Remove the pork from the oven, cover and set aside. Add the stock and port to the sauté pan and deglaze over medium-high heat until the sauce is reduced by half.

◆ Slice the pork a half-inch thick, and serve with port sauce.

HARVEST HINT

Local nuts are difficult to find in the Northeast. One local option is chestnuts; although not widely available they can be found in the fall and early winter at some farmers' markets. If you find chestnuts at the market or if you know where you can find a tree, don't pass them up. Roast chestnuts by scoring an X on the flat side and baking at 350 °F until the shells pull back. Let cool, peel and use or freeze for later use. Chestnuts are lower in fat than most nuts, and are a good source of protein.

Roasted Chicken Legs and Onions with Honey Mustard

4 tablespoons honey

2 teaspoons Dijon-style mustard

½ teaspoon salt

½ teaspoon fresh ground black pepper

4 chicken legs

4 cups onions, sliced

Serves four

◆ Preheat the oven to 350 °F.

◆ In a large bowl, combine the honey, mustard, salt and pepper and mix well. Add the chicken and onions and mix to coat all ingredients.

◆ Remove the chicken legs and place in a roasting pan.

◆ Place the onions on top of the chicken legs.

◆ Roast in the oven for approximately 40 to 50 minutes, until the chicken reaches 165 °F. Serve.

HARVEST HINT

When buying poultry it is important to consider how it was raised and what diet it was fed, so talk with your farmer about their feed practices. Much of our industrially-produced poultry is routinely fed antibiotics to prevent the spread of disease, caused in part by the poor and overcrowded conditions in which the animals are kept. The rampant use of antibiotics in this way reduces its effectiveness in treating illness, and is linked to the increased occurrence of antibiotic resistance in humans.

Harvest-Stuffed Acorn Squash

2 acorn squash, cut in half and
  center cleaned out

¾ cup apple cider

2 tablespoons butter

1 cup onion, chopped

2 tablespoons fresh garlic, chopped

⅔ cup red bell pepper, chopped

1 cup fresh mushrooms, chopped
  (any local variety)

1 cup apple, chopped

2 cups Kale, loosely chopped

1 cup cooked rice (short grain)

¼ teaspoon salt

¼ teaspoon fresh ground black pepper

Serves four

◆ Preheat the oven to 350 °F. Place the squash in a casserole dish, cut side facing up. Pour the cider evenly into the 4 squash halves, and cover the pan. Bake for 60 minutes, or until the squash is fully cooked.

◆ About 15 minutes before the squash is ready, begin preparing the filling. Using a large sauté pan, heat the butter over medium heat. Add the onion and garlic, and sauté for approximately 3 minutes.

◆ Add the red bell pepper, mushrooms and apple to the pan, and cook for another 2 minutes.

◆ Add the kale, cooked rice, salt and pepper and cook until the rice is thoroughly heated and the filling is completely mixed.

◆ Remove the squash from the oven, and discard any remaining cider. Divide the filling mixture into the 4 squash halves, and serve.

HARVEST HINT

Eating meat is a choice that many of us make, but there is an ecological cost associated with it. The production of meat is much more energy intensive than the production of plant-based proteins. If you choose to include meat in your diet, as we do, we suggest making a conscious effort to reduce your ecological impact by eating vegetarian as often as you can, and reducing the portion size when you do eat meat.

Quebec Tortière

Your favorite pie crust, enough for a top
  and bottom layer of a 9 inch pie dish

Filling

¼ pound ground beef

¼ pound ground venison

¼ pound ground buffalo

1 cup onions, chopped

1 tablespoon fresh garlic, chopped

½ teaspoon ground cinnamon

½ teaspoon ground clove

¼ teaspoon salt

¼ teaspoon ground pepper

Milk to brush crust

Pickled Summer Vegetables
  (see page 224 for recipe)

Bread and Butter Pickles
  (see page 226 for recipe)

Serves six (Photo on page 92-93)

◆ Preheat the oven to 400 ºF.

◆ Line the bottom of a pie plate with pie crust and roll out the top crust so that it is ready.

◆ In a large sauté pan, add the beef, venison, buffalo, onions, garlic, cinnamon, clove, salt and pepper. Mix and simmer over low- to medium-heat until the onions are soft and the meat loses its pink color, breaking up the meat as it cooks. It is important that the meat stay moist, so you may have to add a little water while cooking.

◆ When cooked add all of the filling to the pie plate and cover with the top layer of pie crust. Trim the edges if needed, and crimp the upper and lower layers of crust together. Brush the top of the pie lightly with milk.

◆ Bake in the oven for 25 to 30 minutes, until the crust is lightly browned. Keep pie low in the oven to keep the pastry crisp.

◆ Serve with Pickled Summer Vegetables and Bread and Butter Pickles.

HARVEST HINT

Tortière, or meat pie, is a long-standing family dish in Quebec that is often served during the Christmas holiday season. Traditionally it is made from three separate game meats, such as venison, rabbit or moose, but it can also be made with any three varieties of meats, including pork, beef and veal.

PORK ROAST
WITH VERMONT CIDER SAUCE

¼ cup shallots, chopped

2 teaspoons fresh garlic, chopped

1 tablespoon olive oil

2 ½ pounds boneless top loin pork roast

Olive oil, to brush on roast

Salt, to season

Fresh ground black pepper, to season

2 tablespoons bourbon

1 tablespoon cornstarch

½ cup Basic Chicken Stock
   (see page 61 for recipe)

½ cup apple cider

Serves six

◆ Preheat the oven to 375 ºF.

◆ In a searing pan sauté the shallots and garlic in the olive oil over medium heat for approximately 5 minutes or until the onions soften.

◆ Brush olive oil on pork roast, and season with salt and pepper. Add the pork to the pan, and quickly brown all sides of the roast.

◆ Transfer the pan to the oven and cook for approximately 75 minutes, or until the internal temperature of the roast reaches 145 ºF. Remove the roast from the pan, place on a cutting board and cover.

◆ Return the pan to the stovetop over medium heat. Add the bourbon and cook for 1 minute. Whisk the cornstarch into the stock, and add the stock and the cider to the pan, and cook until reduced by half.

◆ To serve, slice the pork half-inch-thick. Serve with the cider sauce.

HARVEST HINT

Apple cider is a quintessential Vermont ingredient. It is produced across the state beginning in early fall, and can be found in the stores and markets through late winter. Try substituting it for orange or other fruit juices, or heat it on the stove for a warm, sweet treat after playing outdoors in the snow.

Braised Turkey Thighs with Currants

⅓ cup all-purpose flour

1 teaspoon salt

1 teaspoon freshly ground black pepper

4 turkey thighs, about 1 pound each,
   rinsed, drained and patted dry

2 tablespoons olive or canola oil

1 cup onion, finely chopped

1 tablespoon fresh garlic, chopped

5 cups turkey or Basic Chicken Stock
   (see page 61 for recipe)

2 tablespoons tomato paste

1 cup dried red currants

¼ cup honey

¼ cup finely fresh parsley, chopped

1 teaspoon fresh sage, finely chopped

Serves six

◆ Combine flour, salt and pepper in a bowl, and mix well.

◆ Place turkey thighs in a bowl and pour the flour mixture over the turkey. Toss until the turkey is well coated with flour. Reserve the remaining flour for later use in the recipe.

◆ Heat a skillet over medium heat, add oil and brown the turkey thighs.

◆ Remove the turkey and set aside. Add the onions and garlic and sauté until tender. Add the reserved flour and cook, stirring until light brown, about 2 minutes.

◆ In a medium bowl combine the stock and tomato paste, and mix well. Add this to the pan and stir in. Return the turkey to the pan, bring to a boil, and then reduce the heat to low. Cover and simmer for 45 to 55 minutes depending on size of the thighs. Cook until the turkey reaches 165 °F.

◆ Add the currants, honey, parsley and sage, and quickly bring to a boil. Reduce heat and simmer for 10 minutes. Serve turkey thighs with sauce.

HARVEST HINT

As a member of a farm share, or if you have your own herb garden, you will have plenty of fresh, flavorful herbs to enjoy all summer long. The key to extending the use of herbs year-round is by freezing, drying, preserving in oil or by bringing some herbs indoors for the winter season. Some of the most successful herbs to bring indoors are rosemary, parsley, thyme and sage.

Stuffed Cabbage
Baked in a Rustic Curried Tomato Sauce

Stuffed Cabbage

4 outer leaves of green cabbage

1 teaspoon olive oil

2 teaspoons fresh garlic, chopped

¼ cup finely red onion, chopped

½ cup mushrooms, chopped

1 cup fresh spinach, chopped (may
   substitute with Swiss chard or Kale)

3 tablespoons Basic Chicken Stock
   (see page 61 for recipe)

¼ teaspoon salt

⅛ teaspoon fresh ground black pepper

1 cup cooked wheat berries

Sauce

1 cup Rustic Homemade Pizza Sauce
   (see page 143 for recipe)

½ cup vegetable or Basic Chicken Stock
   (see page 61 for recipe)

2 teaspoons curry powder

Serves four

◆ Preheat the oven to 350 °F.

◆ Blanch the cabbage leaves in boiling water for about 4 minutes, just until tender. Remove from heat and cool in cold water. Drain and set aside.

◆ In a sauté pan heat the olive oil over medium heat. Add the garlic and onions and sauté for 2 to 3 minutes, stirring.

◆ Add the mushrooms, and sauté for 3 to 4 minutes until the mushrooms are cooked.

◆ Add the spinach, stock, salt and pepper, and cook briefly until the spinach is wilted.

◆ Mix in the wheat berries, remove from heat and set aside.

◆ To stuff the cabbage, pat each leaf dry and lay flat. Fill each with one quarter of the filling. Roll the leaves like an envelope, finishing with a 2-inch by 3-inch log. Arrange all the stuffed cabbage in a casserole dish.

◆ For the sauce combine in a small bowl the Rustic Homemade Tomato Sauce, stock and curry powder and mix well. Pour this sauce over the stuffed cabbage and bake for 35 to 40 minutes. Serve.

"*My mom made two dishes: Take it or Leave it.*"

— *Stephen Wright, Comedian*

PIZZA AND PASTA

Making homemade pasta and pizza dough might seem complicated, but it becomes quite easy once you have a little experience. It is so rewarding to serve your own homemade noodles and sauce, and once you've served fresh pizza you won't go back to take-out. Nourishing whole-wheat flour is our not-so-secret basic ingredient; it gives our pasta, pizza dough and breads a more nutty and complex flavor than using only white flour. With the addition of a few simple ingredients such as seasonal vegetables, locally-produced meats and artisan cheeses, you will be able to prepare an endless variety of satisfying meals at any time of the year.

Pizza and Pasta

NOTE FROM RICHARD — Spring is here and the leaves are busting out, the ground cover is starting to bloom and the wild leeks are coming up. After breakfast we gather our supplies and the dog, and head off into the woods in search of wild leeks. This three to four hour springtime adventure has become a favorite ritual of ours. We search for new patches each year and also return to a few of our special spots. Last year we made are own harvesting tools from maple wood. We spend several hours in the woods until our backpacks are full and our golden retriever is exhausted. When we arrive home, we spend the next several hours cleaning the leeks in cold water, removing roots, dirt and the thin outer layer. We enjoy preparing them for storage in the freezer and also pickling them, but our favorite and most rewarding part of the day is just to eat them, fresh and sautéed in a little butter. The sweet, mild onion flavor comes through and we are always satisfied with our day's harvest.

WILD LEEK AND MUSHROOM RAVIOLI

2 tablespoons olive oil

4 ½ cups mushrooms, chopped
   (may include crimini, shiitake, oyster,
   portabella or any other local
   mushrooms)

2 cups wild leeks, chopped
   (also called ramps)

Pinch of salt

Pinch of fresh ground black pepper

1 ¼ pound batch of whole-wheat pasta
   dough, (see page 138 for recipe)
   seasoned with 1 teaspoon each of
   dried basil, oregano and parsley

Stored Simple Roma Sauce
   (see page 140 for recipe, or other
   homemade tomato sauce)

Serves 4, two large ravioli each

◆ In a large saucepan add the oil and heat over medium-high. Add the mushrooms, leeks, salt and pepper, and cook for approximately 10 minutes, stirring occasionally. Mushrooms should be reduced and most of the liquid evaporated.

◆ Make the pasta dough according to your machine instructions, or follow the recipe for Whole-Wheat Pasta on page 138. Roll out the pasta and lay the sheets on a lightly floured board or other surface. Cut the sheets in half, so that each piece is about 6 inches long and the full width of the roller. You will need at least 4 sheets, or 8 pieces in total.

◆ Divide the cooked mushroom mixture among the 8 pieces of dough. Place the mixture on one side, lightly brush the edges with water and fold the ravioli dough over to form a triangle. Lightly press down along the edges and crimp with a fork.

◆ The ravioli can be cooked immediately, or frozen for later use. To freeze, lightly flour and divide the dough by a layer of wax paper, and store in an airtight container. Cook in lightly boiling water for approximately 5 minutes or until the edges begin to curl. Serve with the last of your frozen Simple Roma Sauce, or your own canned homemade tomato sauce.

HARVEST HINT

Ramps can be found in mixed woodlands with moist soil, and are harvested from April to June in the Northeast. Ramps have a mild onion flavor that is fresh and woody. If ramps are not available, or to use this recipe in other seasons, you can substitute the ramps with green onions. You can extend the availability of ramps by pickling them or making ramp compound butter and freezing it for later use.

WHOLE-WHEAT PASTA

3 cups all-purpose flour

½ cup whole-wheat flour

4 large eggs

2 tablespoons water

½ teaspoon salt

Instructions for making this recipe using a free-standing electric mixer:

◆ In the mixing bowl combine the all-purpose flour, whole-wheat flour, eggs, water and salt. Mix until all ingredients are combined.

◆ Using the dough hook attachment on the mixer, knead for 2 minutes.

◆ Remove dough from bowl and hand knead for 2 minutes. Let the dough rest for 20 minutes. Roll out using the instructions for your pasta maker.

Instructions for making this recipe by hand:

◆ Combine the all-purpose and whole-wheat flours and the salt and place on a cutting board or on the counter. Form a small well in the middle of the flour. In a small bowl beat together the eggs and water. Pour this into the well formed in the flour. Mix the flour into the eggs, working the dough until all flour is mixed in. If the dough is too dry, add 1 tablespoon of water. If the dough is too moist add another tablespoon of flour.

◆ Knead for about 5 minutes or until dough is smooth. Let the dough rest for 20 minutes.

◆ Divide the dough into 4 pieces, and roll out to ⅛-inch thick. Use to make the ravioli, or cut into noodles.

GRILLED STOP LIGHT PEPPER PIZZA

2 tablespoons olive oil

3 tablespoons fresh basil, finely chopped

3 teaspoons fresh garlic, finely chopped

1 large red bell pepper

1 large yellow bell pepper

1 large green bell pepper

Maple Whole-Wheat Pizza Dough
(see page 154 for recipe)

1 cup Rustic Homemade Pizza Sauce
(see page 143 for recipe)

1 ½ cups mozzarella cheese, shredded

Makes one 16-inch pizza

◆ Preheat the oven to 375 °F. Preheat the grill to medium-high.

◆ Combine the olive oil, basil and garlic and mix well; set aside.

◆ To prepare the peppers, cut off the tops, about a half-inch down, and remove seeds. Cut the peppers in halves and place in a large bowl. Add half the oil mixture and toss the peppers until coated. Place the peppers on a hot grill and cook until tender (about 10 minutes), turning peppers every 2 minutes. Set aside and let cool, and then cut into ¼-inch strips and mix the colors together.

◆ Roll out pizza dough to fit your pan or baking stone.

◆ Brush the pizza crust with the remaining olive oil. Spread the pizza sauce on top of pizza, leaving a half-inch around the edges.

◆ Sprinkle the cheese evenly across the pizza. Arrange the peppers on top.

◆ Bake in the oven until the bottom of crust is golden brown, about 15 minutes.

HARVEST HINT

Make this pizza when peppers are plentiful in the garden, and choose whatever mix of colors you prefer or have on hand. If you have extra peppers, we recommend that you grill them following the instructions in this recipe, lay them out on a baking sheet and freeze. Once frozen, remove from baking sheet and store in an airtight bag or container.

SIMPLE ROMA SAUCE

1 tablespoon olive oil

¾ cup onion, chopped

2 tablespoons fresh garlic
  cloves, chopped

12 Roma tomatoes, cored, seeded
  and chopped (about 2 ½ pounds)

1 teaspoon tomato paste

½ tablespoon sugar

⅛ teaspoon salt

⅛ teaspoon fresh ground black pepper

⅛ teaspoon crushed red pepper flakes

¼ cup fresh basil, chopped

Serves four

◆ In a large stainless steel saucepan add the olive oil and onions, and sauté over medium-high heat for approximately 4 minutes. Add the garlic and cook for another minute.

◆ Add to the pan the tomatoes, tomato paste, sugar, salt, pepper and crushed red pepper. Cook, stirring frequently, for 10 minutes. Add the basil, stir in and turn off heat. The sauce should be fairly thick and most of the liquid evaporated.

◆ Serve over your favorite homemade pasta, or pour into pint jars, leaving one inch of space at the top of the jar, and let cool completely before freezing.

HARVEST HINT

This method of making sauce is easier and faster than blanching and peeling the tomatoes. The sauce is much chunkier than a canned bought sauce, and so may not coat the pasta as well. But the flavor of fresh tomatoes is so much better!

EVERY YEAR I FEEL THE NEED TO "SAVE" some of the foods that I have worked hard to put away, like the tomatoes that I have dried or blueberries that I picked last summer, but when the end of winter arrives, I sometimes scramble to use them up so that I don't waste anything! By spring you should have emptied out your freezer, and it's a good time to clean it and have it ready for the next season's bounty.

EGGPLANT, TOMATO AND GREEN ONION PIZZA WITH ROASTED RED PEPPER SAUCE

Maple Whole-Wheat Pizza Dough
  (see page 154 for recipe)
¾ cup roasted red bell pepper
2 cloves fresh garlic
½ teaspoon dried oregano
Olive oil to brush on vegetables
1 eggplant (approximately 1 pound),
  sliced ¼-inch thick lengthwise
8 green onions, ends chopped off
1 ½ cups fresh mozzarella cheese,
  shredded
1 medium tomato, thinly sliced
Fresh ground black pepper

Makes one 16-inch pizza

◆ Preheat the oven to 375 ºF.

◆ Roll out pizza dough to fit your pan or baking stone.

◆ In a food processor add the red bell pepper, garlic and oregano and process until smooth. Set aside.

◆ Preheat grill to medium-high. Lightly brush olive oil onto the eggplant and green onions. Grill the eggplant until just browned, turning once. Grill the green onions quickly, being careful not to burn. Once cooked, remove the eggplant and onions from grill and set aside.

◆ Cut the eggplant to about 1-inch square, and cut the onions to about 1 inch long.

◆ Spread the red pepper sauce across the top of pizza to cover, leaving a half-inch around the edges. Arrange the eggplant and onions evenly on the pizza.

◆ Sprinkle the cheese evenly on the pizza. Arrange the sliced tomatoes evenly on top of the cheese. Season with pepper.

◆ Bake in the oven until the bottom of the crust is golden brown, about 15 minutes.

HARVEST HINT

A roasted red bell pepper sauce is a spicy change from the usual tomato sauce. Use frozen roasted red bell peppers to make this sauce throughout the winter.

Rustic Homemade Pizza Sauce

2 tablespoons olive oil

¼ cup onion, minced

3 teaspoons fresh garlic, minced

6 cups fresh tomato, cored,
  seeded and quartered

¼ cup tomato paste

3 tablespoons balsamic vinegar

3 teaspoons of dried basil

2 teaspoons dried oregano

1 teaspoon dried parsley

⅛ tsp crushed red pepper flakes

Makes sauce for three 16-inch pizzas
  (about 3 ½ cups)

◆ Heat the olive oil over medium-low heat. Add the onions and garlic and sauté about 5 to 7 minutes, or until tender.

◆ Add the tomatoes, paste, vinegar, basil, oregano, parsley and pepper flakes and simmer for 45 minutes, or until quite thick and liquid is cooked off.

◆ Purée the mixture in a food processor until smooth and use, or freeze for use during the winter.

HARVEST HINT

Homemade pizza can be a nutritious meal and a fun family tradition. Homemade pizza sauce like this one is lower in salt and sugar than purchased sauce, and the flavor is incomparable. Have the family participate by rolling the dough, choosing and chopping their toppings and creating their own custom pizzas.

DUCK RAGOÛT

1 fresh duck, approximately 6 pounds

1 medium onion, skin on, sliced in half

1 small carrot

Water to cover duck carcass

2 tablespoons duck fat,
   reserved from above

1 cup chopped onion, chopped

1 tablespoon fresh garlic, chopped

5 small carrots, peeled and chopped
   (about 1 ½ cups)

2 parsnips, peeled and chopped

1 tablespoon fresh oregano leaves
   (or 1 teaspoon dried)

¼ teaspoon crushed red pepper

⅛ teaspoon salt

⅛ teaspoon fresh ground black pepper

Fresh Parmesan, grated

Serves six

◆ Preheat the oven to 375 °F.

◆ Place the duck in a roasting pan and cook for approximately 20 minutes per pound, until the internal temperature of the thickest part of the bird reaches 165 °F. Let cool enough to handle.

◆ De-bone the duck, tearing into pieces that are bite-size. Refrigerate the duck meat. Reserve 2 tablespoons of fat from the pan.

◆ Put the carcass in a stock pot. Add the 2 onion halves, whole carrot and water to cover the carcass. Simmer for at least 90 minutes.

◆ Heat a heavy saucepan over medium heat, add duck fat and melt. Add the onions and sauté until tender.

◆ Add the garlic and cook another 2 minutes.

◆ Add the duck meat, carrots, parsnips, oregano, crushed red pepper and 2 cups of duck stock. Simmer for 60 minutes, adding more stock as needed to maintain a thick liquid consistency.

◆ Add salt and pepper to taste.

◆ Serve over orecchiette or any type of pasta. Serve with grated fresh Parmesan.

HARVEST HINT

Fall is a perfect time for a meal made with local duck, especially if you have a waterfowl hunter in your family. Duck is a good substitute for chicken and turkey in many recipes, and offers a very rich, complex flavor.

FRESH ARUGULA AND VERMONT FETA PIZZA

Maple Whole-Wheat Pizza Dough
  (see page 154 for recipe)

2 tablespoons olive oil

1 tablespoon plus 1 teaspoon
  garlic, finely chopped

3 cups arugula, roughly chopped,
  lightly packed

½ cup dried cured olives, with pits
  removed and cut in half

½ cup red onion, sliced

1 cup fresh feta cheese, shredded
  or crumbled

½ cup fresh mozzarella cheese,
  shredded

Makes one 16-inch pizza

◆ Preheat the oven to 375 °F.

◆ Roll out pizza dough to fit your pan or baking stone.

◆ In a small bowl, combine the olive oil and garlic. Using a pastry brush, brush the oil mixture on the top of pizza, leaving a half-inch around the edges.

◆ Arrange the arugula, olives and onion evenly on the pizza.

◆ Sprinkle the feta and mozzarella cheeses evenly on the pizza. Bake in the oven until the bottom of the crust is golden brown, about 15 minutes.

HARVEST HINT

The traditional style of making feta cheese is to use sheep or goat's milk and age for six months in salt brine. There is a good variety of locally made feta cheeses that are produced in this traditional manner. The larger commercial producers make the cheese with cow's milk, which results in a milder, less distinct flavor.

Spinach, Mushroom and Caramelized Onion Pizza

Maple Whole-Wheat Pizza Dough
  (see page 154 for recipe)

1 tablespoon olive oil

1 medium onion, sliced

2 tablespoons Fresh Basil Pesto
  (see page 221 for recipe)

2 cups fresh spinach, chopped

1 cup mushrooms, very thinly sliced

1 ½ cups mozzarella cheese, shredded

Makes one 16-inch pizza

◆ Preheat the oven to 375 °F.

◆ Roll out pizza dough to fit your pan or baking stone.

◆ Heat the olive oil in a small sauté pan over medium-high heat.

◆ Add the onions and cook for 10 minutes. Reduce heat to low and cook for 30 minutes, stirring occasionally. Let cool.

◆ Brush the pizza crust with the pesto, leaving a half-inch around the edges uncovered.

◆ Arrange the cooked onions, spinach and mushrooms evenly on the pizza and sprinkle the cheese evenly on top.

◆ Bake in the oven until the bottom of crust is golden brown, about 15 minutes.

NOTE FROM RICHARD— It was a typical, cold late February day when I was picking up my farm share. I was suffering from the butternut blues; that feeling of being "squashed" when it comes to the last couple weeks of the winter share. When I walked into the barn I was surprised to see the first of the over-wintered spinach. Seeing the spinach energized my enthusiasm for fresh vegetables. And it wasn't just me that was surprised; each time someone new came in I heard, "wow, spinach!" It was a treat that lasted until the winter share was over. Now I know the feeling that Popeye gets when he sees that dark green, leafy vegetable that we disliked as kids. Fresh spinach will cure the butternut blues!

EGGPLANT TOMATO SAUCE

2 tablespoons olive oil

1 cup red onion, chopped

3 large fresh garlic cloves,
    peeled and chopped

6 small to medium tomatoes, chopped

1 large eggplant, peeled and
    cubed ½-inch

2 cups homemade tomato sauce
    (you can use your own recipe)

¼ cup red wine

1 tablespoon sugar

1 tablespoon fresh parsley, chopped

2 tablespoons fresh basil, chopped

1 teaspoon Italian seasoning

¼ teaspoon crushed red pepper

¼ teaspoon salt

Fresh ground black pepper to taste

Makes two quarts

◆ In a heavy saucepan heat olive oil over medium heat. Add onions and sauté until soft, approximately 5 minutes.

◆ Add the garlic and cook another minute, stirring.

◆ Add the tomatoes, eggplant, tomato sauce, wine, sugar, parsley, basil, Italian seasoning, crushed red pepper, salt and pepper. Simmer uncovered for 2 hours, stirring occasionally. When ready, eggplant should be soft but still formed.

◆ Serve over whole-wheat pasta or cooked wheat berries, or freeze for later use.

HARVEST HINT

If you have children who love spaghetti but might not be interested in eating eggplant, purée the sauce at the end of the cooking time using a hand-held immersion blender or food processor. If you don't have homemade tomato sauce but have lots of tomatoes, substitute the sauce with one recipe of tomato juice (see page 43 for recipe).

Woodland Mushrooms with Black Pepper Fettuccine

¼ cup dried mushrooms, chopped

1 cup Basic Chicken Stock,
 (see page 61 for recipe)

1 tablespoon olive oil

⅓ cup onion, chopped

1 teaspoon fresh garlic, chopped

2 ½ cups assorted local mushrooms,
 sliced (may include crimini,
 shitake, oyster, portabella or
 any other local mushrooms)

1 tablespoon all-purpose flour

2 tablespoons bourbon

½ cup dried tomatoes, sliced

4 tablespoons crème fraîche

2 tablespoons fresh parsley, chopped

Salt and pepper, to taste

¾ pound fresh Black Pepper Fettuccine
 (see page 149 for recipe)

Serves four

◆ In a small bowl, add the dried mushrooms to the stock and let soak for at least 15 minutes.

◆ In a saucepan heat the olive oil over medium heat, add onion and garlic, and cook for approximately 5 minutes or until onions begin to soften and are lightly browned.

◆ Add the fresh mushrooms to the pan and continue to cook for 5 minutes.

◆ Add the flour to the pan, and stir until completely dissolved; do not brown.

◆ Add the bourbon to the mushrooms in the saucepan, and cook, stirring, for 1 minute.

◆ Add the stock and rehydrated mushrooms, and cook until reduced by half, stirring occasionally.

◆ Bring water to boil to cook the fettuccine. Add the fettuccine to the boiling water and cook until al dente.

◆ Add the tomatoes and crème fraîche to the pan, and stir until completely mixed and sauce begins to thicken.

◆ Stir in the parsley. Add salt and pepper to taste. Drain the cooked pasta, and add to the saucepan. Toss to coat pasta with sauce, and serve.

HARVEST HINT

Drying removes the moisture from food so that bacteria cannot grow and spoil the food during storage. Drying foods intensifies the flavor, no matter what fruit or vegetable you dry. We recommend drying cherry tomatoes during the height of the harvest season; the result has such concentrated flavor and is so sweet you will eat it like candy. We also recommend that if you are going to dry your own food that you use a food dehydrator.

BLACK PEPPER FETTUCCINE

3 cups all-purpose flour

½ cup whole-wheat flour

4 large eggs

2 tablespoons cracked black pepper

2 tablespoons water

1 tablespoon olive oil

½ teaspoon salt

Instructions for making this recipe using a free-standing electric mixer:

◆ In mixing bowl combine the all-purpose flour, whole-wheat flour, eggs, pepper, water, oil and salt. Mix until all ingredients are combined. Using the dough hook attachment on the mixer, knead for 2 minutes.

◆ Remove dough from bowl and hand-knead for 2 minutes. Let the dough rest for 20 minutes.

◆ Roll out using the instructions for your pasta maker.

Instructions for making this recipe by hand:

◆ Combine the all-purpose and whole-wheat flours, salt and pepper, and place on a cutting board or on the counter. Form a small well in the middle of the flour. In a small bowl beat together the eggs, water and oil. Pour this into the well formed in the flour. Mix the flour into the eggs, working the dough until all flour is mixed in. If the dough is too dry, add 1 tablespoon of water. If the dough is too moist add another tablespoon of flour.

◆ Knead for about 5 minutes or until dough is smooth. Let the dough rest for 20 minutes.

◆ Divide the dough into 4 pieces, and roll out to ⅛-inch thick. Using a knife or pizza cutter, cut into noodles that are approximately 12-inches long and ⅓-inch wide. If freezing for later use, lightly flour the pasta and freeze in single portion sizes.

FARMS AND THE ENVIRONMENT

In terms of environmental impact, buying from small local farms is perhaps the most significant decision that we, the consumer, can make. In general, small farms use more sustainable farming practices than the mega-farms that are spread out across the country. Even small farms that are not certified organic are likely to use fewer pesticides, and many do not routinely administer antibiotics to their stock. A healthy family farm is one that uses its natural resources, including their land and livestock, in a sustainable fashion.

"When tillage begins, other arts follow. The farmers, therefore, are the founders of human civilization."

— Daniel A. Webster

LOCAL ECONOMIES AND FOOD

YOU CAN BUY ANYTHING YOU NEED AT THE SUPER-MARKET, at any time of year.

Buying instead from a local farmer, whether it is from a farm stand, a farmers' market or through community supported agriculture (CSA), ensures that money goes directly to the farmer.

This means that the farmer is paid a higher price for the products than if he sold through a distributor. Financial success means that the he or she is more likely to continue farming, now and in future generations.

Many consumers have no idea how or where their food is grown; buying locally can provide that missing connection.

There is also a positive impact on the community at large when you purchase food locally. For example, if Vermonters shifted just 10% of their food purchases to locally grown food products it would add more than $100 million to the state's economy. Similar effects would be seen across the Northeast.

"How better than to support the health of the community than to bring something healthy like a farmers' market to our backyard."
— Avtar Nijjer-Sidhu

Golden Tomato Pizza with Pesto and Kale

Maple Whole-Wheat Pizza Dough
(see page 154 for recipe)
2 cubes basil pesto, thawed (equivalent
to 3 tablespoons) (see page 221
for recipe)
1 tablespoon olive oil
1 tablespoon fresh garlic, chopped
3 cups kale, roughly chopped,
lightly packed
¾ cup dried cherry tomatoes,
preferably Sun Gold
¼ cup onion, chopped
1 ½ cups fresh mozzarella cheese,
shredded
Fresh ground black pepper

Makes one 16-inch pizza
(Photo on page 92-93)

◆ Preheat the oven to 375 °F.

◆ Roll out pizza dough to fit your pan or baking stone.

◆ Spread the pesto on top of pizza to cover, leaving a half-inch around the edges.

◆ In a sauté pan, add the olive oil, garlic and kale, and sauté over medium heat for about 10 minutes or until kale begins to soften slightly. In the last minute of cooking stir in the cherry tomatoes.

◆ Arrange the kale and tomato mixture evenly on the pizza. Arrange the onion on top.

◆ Sprinkle the cheese over the top of the pizza. Be careful to cover the tomatoes and kale with cheese or they may burn during baking. Season with pepper.

◆ Bake in the oven until the bottom of the crust is golden brown, about 15 minutes

HARVEST HINT

Another useful way to use dried tomatoes is to make tomato pesto. In a food processor, simply combine dried tomatoes, garlic, olive oil, salt and pepper, and process until smooth. Use tomato pesto as a base for pizza, a light sauce for pasta or as a spread.

LAMB SAUSAGE AND ROASTED GARLIC PIZZA

Sausage

¾ pound or 1½ cups ground lamb

4 cloves garlic, chopped fine

1 tablespoon parsley, chopped

¼ teaspoon fennel seeds

Pizza

Maple Whole-Wheat Pizza Dough
   (see page 154 for recipe)

1 cup Rustic Homemade Pizza Sauce
   (see page 143 for recipe)

1 ½ cups mozzarella cheese, shredded

1 recipe of Lamb Sausage, cooked
   and sliced

½ cup red onion, chopped

1 whole head of garlic, roasted and
   separated from the white membranes
   and coarsely chopped

3 tablespoons fresh basil, chopped

Makes one 16-inch pizza

◆ To make the sausage, combine the ground lamb, garlic, parsley and fennel seeds in a bowl and mix, using your hands, until well blended.

◆ If you don't have a sausage maker, hand shape the sausage mixture into links about 4-inches long and about 1-inch thick. If you have a sausage maker, use pork casing to make the sausages.

◆ Cook sausage in a saucepan over low heat until firm, about 15 to 20 minutes.

◆ Preheat the oven to 375 °F.

◆ Roll out pizza dough to fit your pan or baking stone.

◆ Spread the pizza sauce across the top of pizza to cover, leaving a half-inch around the edges.

◆ Sprinkle the cheese evenly on the pizza. Arrange the sliced sausage, red onion, garlic and basil on top of the pizza.

◆ Bake in the oven until the bottom of the crust is golden brown, about 15 minutes.

HARVEST HINT

There is no substitute for fresh garlic. In the early fall start looking at the farmers' market for hand-braided garlic. Hang the braids in a dry spot close to the kitchen for convenience, and snip off one head at a time as you need it. I buy at least two braids every year, knowing that I don't want to run out mid-winter!

MAPLE WHOLE-WHEAT PIZZA DOUGH

1 tablespoon maple syrup

¾ cup water, at 100 to 110 °F

1 tablespoon active dry yeast

½ cup whole-wheat flour

1 ¾ cups all-purpose flour

   (¼ cup set aside)

½ teaspoon salt

1 tablespoon olive oil

Cornmeal for pan

Makes one 16-inch pizza

◆ In a large bowl add the maple syrup, water and yeast. Mix slightly until dissolved and let stand for 5 minutes to let the yeast develop.

◆ In another bowl combine the whole-wheat flour, all-purpose flour (less ¼ cup) and salt. Sift together with a fork.

◆ When the yeast is ready add the olive oil and the larger amount of flour, and mix until well blended and dough begins to form.

◆ Place on a clean counter and knead dough, adding the ¼ cup flour a little at a time until combined. The dough should be firm and able to form a ball. Place the dough back in the bowl and let rise for 45 minutes.

◆ Roll out dough and place on pizza pan or stone. For a slightly crisper crust, sprinkle the pizza pan or stone lightly with cornmeal. Follow baking directions in specific pizza recipes.

HARVEST HINT

Your whole family will love this pizza dough. It is slightly crisp with a bit of a nutty taste and a hint of sweetness. Whole-wheat flour is milled from the entire wheat grain, including the bran and the germ, which is removed in the milling of white flour. For better nutrition, experiment by substituting whole-wheat flour for some of the white flour in your favorite recipes. Flour can go rancid so store it in a cool, dark place or even in the freezer.

FOCACCIA

1 cup water at 100 to 110 °F

1½ teaspoons active dry yeast

1 teaspoon maple syrup

2 cups all-purpose flour
  (¼ cup set aside)

1 cup whole-wheat flour

1½ teaspoons salt

¼ cup olive oil

Cornmeal for pan

Serves four

◆ In a large bowl add the water, yeast and maple syrup. Mix together, and let sit for 5 minutes until yeast is dissolved.

◆ In a medium bowl combine the all-purpose flour (less ¼ cup), the whole-wheat flour and salt. Mix together.

◆ When the yeast is ready add the olive oil and flour mixture and mix until well blended and dough begins to form. Place the dough on a clean, a lightly-floured counter. Knead the dough, adding the ¼ cup flour a little at a time, until all the flour is mixed and dough is firm. Form a ball with the dough, and place back in bowl. Cover with a clean towel and let rise for 60 minutes.

◆ Lightly oil a 12-inch by 9-inch pan, and sprinkle cornmeal in the pan. Lay the dough in the pan and, using your hands, work the dough out towards the sides of the pan. Cover and let rise again for another 30 minutes. Preheat the oven to 450 °F.

◆ Bake for 22 minutes or until golden brown. Remove from the oven, take out of the pan and let cool on a wire rack.

HARVEST HINT

Focaccia is one of our favorite breads to make, and this recipe is simple. There are many variations that can be made using this recipe. Simply brush the top of the focaccia with oil, sprinkle with fresh rosemary, roasted onion and garlic, dried tomatoes or any fresh ingredients that you like. This step should be done just before the last rising of the dough.

WHOLE-WHEAT BREAD
WITH OATS AND FLAX

1 cup plus 2 tablespoons water, at 110 ºF

4 tablespoons olive oil

2 cups whole-wheat flour

1 cup bread flour

¾ cup rolled oats

3 tablespoons brown sugar

2 tablespoons ground flax seed

1 ¼ teaspoon salt

1 tablespoon powdered buttermilk

2 ½ teaspoons active dry yeast

Cornmeal for pan

Makes one loaf

◆ Combine the water, olive oil, whole-wheat and bread flour, oats, sugar, flax seed, salt, powdered buttermilk and yeast in a mixing bowl. Knead dough until it forms a ball and pulls away from the sides of the bowl.

◆ Cover bowl with a cloth and let rise for approximately 90 minutes or until it has doubled in size.

◆ Form bread into a loaf about 8 inches long. Place on a lightly greased sheet pan that has been sprinkled with cornmeal. If you prefer you may use parchment paper instead.

◆ Let bread rise again until doubled in size, approximately 90 minutes.

◆ Approximately 30 minutes before the bread will be baked, preheat the oven to 375 º F. Bake the bread in the oven for 25 to 30 minutes or until the internal temperature reaches 195 ºF. Remove from oven and let rest for 30 minutes.

HARVEST HINT

Hands down the best thing about baking bread is the aroma when it first comes out of the oven. And next is the pleasure of slicing off a piece of warm bread and slathering it with fresh butter. Baking homemade bread in the winter has a side benefit of warming your house as it bakes, and it can be done at your leisure. When you make your own bread you can control the quality by choosing local ingredients, like butter, grains, dried fruits and dairy products.

MULTIGRAIN CRISPS

⅓ cup cornmeal

⅓ cup whole-wheat flour

⅓ cup all-purpose flour

¼ cup King Arthur Flour Harvest
   Grains Blend

⅓ cup Tarentaise cheese, shredded

¼ cup plus 1 tablespoon water

1 tablespoon olive oil

1 teaspoon baking powder

¼ teaspoon salt

◆ Preheat the oven to 375 °F.

◆ In a free-standing electric mixer bowl, combine the cornmeal, whole-wheat and all-purpose flour, Harvest Grains, cheese, water, olive oil, baking powder and salt. Mix on low until the mixture begins to ball.

◆ On the counter or a wooden cutting board roll the mixture out as thin as possible, approximately ⅛-inch thick. Place on parchment paper, and using a pizza cutter, cut into squares. Lay the parchment and crisps on a baking stone or a baking sheet.

◆ Bake for 10 minutes or until slightly crisp. Turn over and bake for another 10 minutes.

◆ Remove and cool on a wire rack. Serve within a day or two for best quality.

HARVEST HINT

While the ingredients in homemade crackers may not be all local, making crackers at home is easy, saves money and is good for the environment because of the packaging and shipping avoided. Crackers are notoriously high in fat (especially saturated) and sodium; you can control both by making your own.

FARM ROOTS

From the farmers' fields we gathered our roots to create a variety of fresh side dishes that you can enjoy in the changing seasons. In the Northeast there is a plentiful supply of produce available year round and we have created some unique combinations of vegetables, herbs and fruit in these recipes. If you enjoy eating vegetarian, these recipes are hearty enough to serve as a main meal, or complement any of the entrée recipes. Eating more local vegetables in your daily diet is good for your health and has less of an impact on the environment than eating meat. As you use the recipes to guide you through the seasons, you will find that there is an abundance of vegetables and variety at the farmers' markets. The opportunity to preserve the harvest only comes once a season, so be prepared to preserve some of your favorite foods for the winter season or when you desire the flavors of another season's harvest.

Farm Roots

Spring Asparagus with Garden Peas and Wheat Berries

¾ cup wheat berries, rinsed

1 tablespoon olive oil

1 cup onion, finely chopped

1 teaspoon fresh garlic, minced

8 stalks fresh asparagus

1 cup frozen peas (you can use up
what you have in the freezer)

2 tablespoons fresh parsley, chopped

1 tablespoon fresh Parmesan cheese,
grated

1 tablespoon balsamic vinegar

Fresh ground black pepper,
to taste

Serves four

◆ In a large saucepan add the wheat berries to 4 cups of water. Bring to a boil for 2 minutes, then reduce heat, cover and simmer for 75 minutes.

◆ In a small saucepan, heat the olive oil over medium heat. Add the onion and garlic and sauté approximately 7 minutes, until lightly browned. Remove from heat and reserve.

◆ Trim the bottom ends of the asparagus and cut each stalk into 4 pieces.

◆ In the last 5 minutes of cooking the wheat berries, add the asparagus and peas to the saucepan.

◆ Drain the wheat berry and vegetable mixture. Toss in a bowl with the onion and garlic mixture, parsley, Parmesan, vinegar and pepper. Serve.

HARVEST HINT

This recipe serves a generous portion of one cup each, so if you have any left, it makes a wonderful cold salad.

ASPARAGUS BROILED IN HONEY
AND BALSAMIC VINEGAR

20 stalks fresh asparagus, washed
  and bottom-inch removed

1 teaspoon olive oil

1 teaspoon honey

1 teaspoon balsamic vinegar

½ teaspoon fresh lemon juice

Salt and fresh ground black pepper,
  to taste

Serves four

◆ Preheat the broiler.

◆ Place the asparagus in a shallow baking pan.

◆ In a small bowl, whisk together the olive oil, honey, vinegar and lemon juice, and pour over the asparagus. Sprinkle salt and pepper over the asparagus.

◆ Broil on the top rack of the oven for 5 to 8 minutes, or until asparagus is caramelized and tender.

◆ Serve topped with any of the remaining dressing in the pan.

HARVEST HINT

To keep asparagus fresh, store it in the refrigerator standing upright in one inch of water. Wide-mouth canning jars work perfectly for this job.

SAUTÉED SUMMER SQUASH WITH
RED ONION AND DILL

2 teaspoons olive oil

¾ cup red onion, julienne

3 cups yellow squash, julienne

3 ½ tablespoons fresh dill, chopped

Salt and fresh ground black pepper
  to season

Serves four

◆ In a medium sauté pan, add oil and heat to medium.

◆ Add the red onion and sauté for 3 minutes.

◆ Add the squash and sauté for 5 to 6 minutes.

◆ Add dill, salt and pepper, and sauté for 2 more minutes. Remove from heat and serve.

PARMESAN-CRUSTED TOMATO PUDDING

3 cups fresh tomato, cubed,
  including juices

1 cup French bread, cubed
  (or any crusty bread)

¼ cup white onion, chopped

2 cloves fresh garlic, chopped

1 tablespoon fresh basil, chopped

1 teaspoon olive oil

⅛ teaspoon salt

⅛ teaspoon fresh ground black pepper

3 teaspoons Parmesan cheese, grated
  (or any hard grating cheese)

3 teaspoons homemade
  fresh bread crumbs

Serves four

◆ Preheat oven to 350 °F.

◆ In a large bowl combine tomato and juices, bread, onion, garlic, basil, olive oil, salt and pepper, and mix well. Mixture should be quite wet.

◆ Lightly brush a casserole dish with olive oil. Spread the mixture evenly in the dish.

◆ Sprinkle the top of the casserole with Parmesan cheese and bread crumbs.

◆ Place in the oven and bake for 20 minutes, until thickened and top is lightly browned. Remove from oven and serve.

NOTE FROM RICHARD — My wife and I frequently drive to Montreal for dinner, and on one such trip in late summer we visited one of our favorite restaurants. We noticed a new shrimp dish on the menu and it came with tomato pudding. Since neither of us had ever heard the term "pudding" used with tomatoes, we ordered it to share. The tomato pudding was a delicious blend of tomatoes, garlic, basil and sourdough bread, baked in a casserole dish. The top of the pudding was crusted with Parmesan cheese, and it was surrounded with shrimp. We enjoyed the tomato pudding so much that we decided to make it at home as a side dish. We enjoy making it when tomatoes are at their peak of harvest and, also with the frozen tomatoes that we preserve over the summer; either way this dish has become a regular favorite of ours.

DAD'S BARBEQUE POTATOES

3 pounds potatoes, peeled
  and sliced thick

½ pound onions, peeled and sliced

2 tablespoons fresh garlic, chopped

3 tablespoons butter

1 tablespoon olive oil

1 cup water

Salt and fresh ground black pepper,
  to taste

Serves four

◆ Preheat the grill to approximately 300 ºF (not higher).

◆ In a heavy stainless steel or cast iron pan that has a fitted lid, add the potatoes, onions, garlic, butter, olive oil and water, and stir to mix.

◆ Cover and cook slowly on the grill, stirring occasionally, for approximately 90 to 120 minutes, or until potatoes have softened.

◆ Remove the lid and cook another 30 minutes or until the sides of the pan and some of the potatoes begin to brown lightly. Add the salt and pepper, and serve.

NOTE FROM DIANE— This recipe has been a family favorite since my childhood. These are Dad's potatoes, cooked slowly on the grill, and they taste like no other potatoes I have ever had. The flavor and texture is somewhere between mashed and scalloped, yet is altogether different. Years ago we had a large family reunion at our camp, with guests coming from hours away and staying all weekend. Two of us peeled potatoes for hours to get ready. We had so many potatoes that we brought them to a neighbor's house to slice, using her food processor. Finally we put them on the wood fire to cook, alongside the roast pig. We cooked over fifty pounds of potatoes and there wasn't a bite left at the end of the day.

Olive and Basil Stuffed Plum Tomatoes

6 medium size plum tomatoes

1 ¼ cup fresh bread crumbs,
  coarsely chopped

¼ cup onion, finely chopped

¼ cup sliced black olives

3 tablespoons fresh basil, chopped

2 tablespoons fresh parsley, chopped

1 tablespoon garlic, finely chopped

½ tablespoon fresh thyme leaves

¼ teaspoon fresh ground black pepper

¼ cup Parmesan cheese, grated

3 tablespoons olive oil

Serves six

◆ Preheat the oven to 375 °F.

◆ Wash the tomatoes and cut in half, length-wise.

◆ Notch out the top core of the tomatoes. With a spoon, hollow out the tomatoes by removing the seeds and membrane around them, creating a bowl for the filling ingredients.

◆ In a large bowl, combine the bread crumbs, onion, olives, basil, parsley, garlic, thyme and pepper and mix well.

◆ Mix in the Parmesan cheese and olive oil.

◆ Stuff the tomatoes with the mixture so it is mounded over the top and place on a non-reactive baking pan. Continue until all the tomatoes are stuffed and all of the filling is used.

◆ Bake in the oven for approximately 15 to 20 minutes, or until the tomatoes are tender and the filling is golden brown. Serve.

HARVEST HINT

If you have bread that isn't quite fresh enough for a sandwich, wrap it tightly and store it in your freezer. It can be used to make great comfort foods like bread pudding or stuffing, or have a second life as garlic croutons to perk up soup or salad, or simply become homemade bread crumbs.

MAPLE GINGER ROASTED BUTTERNUT SQUASH

1 large butternut squash, peeled,
cleaned and cubed half-inch

1 tablespoon olive oil

1 clove fresh garlic, chopped

1 teaspoon fresh ginger, chopped

¼ teaspoon fresh ground black pepper

1 tablespoon maple syrup

Serves six

◆ Preheat the oven to 375 ºF.

◆ Toss the squash with the olive oil, and put into a roasting pan.

◆ Bake the squash in the oven for 30 minutes, stirring once.

◆ Add the garlic, ginger and pepper, and continue to bake 15 to 25 minutes, or until tender but not overcooked. The squash should be firm enough to maintain its shape.

◆ Remove from the oven. Stir in the maple syrup and serve.

HARVEST HINT

If you have a winter farm share, you are certain to receive an abundance of winter squash. When cooking squash, conserve energy by doubling this recipe (but cook each batch in separate pans). You can use the extra batch in the Rockville Market Hash recipe, or freeze. Don't forget to save the seeds for roasting, or for sharing with the birds.

Sweet Cinnamon Delicata Squash with Apple

2 delicata squash

2 tablespoons butter

1 ½ cups apple, shredded

2 tablespoons honey

½ teaspoon ground cinnamon

Serves four

◆ Preheat the oven to 350 °F.

◆ Cut squash in half, length-wise, and scoop out the seeds. Place in shallow baking pan with enough water to cover the bottom of the pan. Bake for 20 to 30 minutes. Pierce with a paring knife to test tenderness. When cooked remove from the oven and set aside for 2 minutes to rest.

◆ Heat a sauté pan over medium heat, add the butter and melt. Add the apple and sauté for 2 minutes. Add honey and cinnamon and mix in well. Remove from heat.

◆ When squash has cooled slightly, scoop out the meat from the outer shell of the squash and add it to the apple mixture. Stir until thoroughly mixed. Reheat just before serving.

HARVEST HINT

Delicata squash, also known as Bohemian squash, is found in many local farmers' markets from mid-August until December. It ranges in color anywhere from green to orange, is oblong in shape and has an average weight of 1 to 2 pounds each. Once cooked, the flesh inside is yellow and firm in texture with a sweet taste.

ONE IMPORTANT REASON to buy your food locally is for good nutrition. Research shows that our food supply, particularly produce, is less nutritious than it was decades ago. This means that we are consuming fewer nutrients per dollar spent on groceries. In particular, organic vegetables are shown to have a higher nutrient density than their conventionally grown counterparts, so although it might appear that organic (or organically grown) vegetables are pricey—you may be getting more for your money.

ROASTED AUTUMN HODGEPODGE

2 parsnips, peeled and sliced
   (about 1 cup)

1 large carrot, peeled and sliced
   (about 1 cup)

½ turnip, peeled and cubed
   (about 1 ½ cups)

4 cloves fresh garlic, peeled
   and cut in half

2 tablespoons olive oil

2 teaspoons fresh rosemary
   leaves, chopped

1 cup Brussels sprouts, peeled and
   washed (cut in half if very large)

1 leek, washed and cut in half
   lengthwise, and chopped into
   1-inch pieces

Fresh ground black pepper, to taste

Serves four

◆ Preheat oven to 375 °F.

◆ In a roasting pan combine the parsnip, carrot, turnip, garlic, olive oil and rosemary, and toss to coat the vegetables.

◆ Cook vegetables in the oven for 30 minutes, stirring occasionally.

◆ Add the Brussels sprouts and leeks, stir in and continue cooking another 15 minutes, or until all the vegetables are tender and beginning to brown.

◆ Remove from oven, add the pepper and serve.

HARVEST HINT

This recipe works well using any fall root vegetables, including rutabaga, onions, potatoes or celeriac.
While this is described as a fall recipe, it is a comforting way to prepare and eat vegetables all through the winter.

SMOKEY CIDER BRAISED BRUSSELS SPROUTS

2 slices bacon, chopped

⅔ cup onion, chopped

¾ pound Brussels sprouts, peeled,
  washed, and quartered

⅔ cup apple cider

⅔ cup fresh apple, chopped

Serves four

◆ In a saucepan, cook the bacon over medium heat until just crispy. Add the onions and sauté for 2 minutes, until just beginning to soften and lightly brown.

◆ Add the Brussels sprouts and sauté for 3 minutes, until lightly browned.

◆ Lower the heat to medium-low, add the cider and cover. Cook for 8 minutes. Stir in the apples and cook for 2 more minutes. Serve.

HARVEST HINT

Brussels sprouts can be left in the garden until there is snow on the ground, well into October and November or even beyond. They are best purchased while still on the stalk; simply cut the sprouts from the stalk as they are needed. Eat them quickly as the flavor intensifies when they are stored.

ROCKVILLE MARKET HASH

1 tablespoon olive oil

¼ cup onion, chopped

2 cups butternut squash,
  diced and cooked

1 cup red potato, cooked and diced

A pinch of salt

A pinch of fresh ground black pepper

1 tablespoon fresh parsley, chopped

Serves four

◆ In a large sauté pan heat the olive oil over medium heat, add the onion and cook for 2 minutes.

◆ Add the squash and potato, and sauté for 8 to 10 minutes or until the mixture starts to brown.

◆ Remove from heat, stir in the salt, pepper and parsley, and serve.

We both enjoy visiting our local farms, and writing this book gave us a great excuse to do so. One of our first visits was to Rockville Market Farm, in Starksboro, Vermont, where Eric and Keenan Rozendaal grow winter squash, among other crops. It is humbling to see the amount of work and resources needed to produce our food. Farming is a way of life, and I envy those who choose this as their life's work. It seems that it must be intensely satisfying to know that your harvest will nourish others.

GOLDEN SPAGHETTI SQUASH
WITH SAUTÉED FENNEL

1 spaghetti squash

1 tablespoon olive oil

½ cup fennel, shaved thin

¼ cup onion, chopped

2 teaspoons fresh garlic, minced

Salt and fresh ground
   black pepper to taste

Serves four

◆ Preheat the oven to 350 °F.

◆ Cut squash in half, length-wise, and scoop out the seeds. Place squash in a shallow baking pan with enough water to cover the bottom of the pan. Bake for 20 to 30 minutes. Pierce with a paring knife to test tenderness. When cooked, remove from the oven and set aside for 2 minutes to cool slightly. Scoop the meat from the outer shell of the squash. Set aside 2 cups of squash for later use in this recipe.

◆ In a sauté pan heat the olive oil over medium heat. Add the fennel, onions and garlic, and sauté for 3 to 4 minutes until fennel is tender.

◆ Add the squash to the fennel and reduce heat to low. Sauté for 5 more minutes. Add salt and pepper and serve.

HARVEST HINT

Spaghetti squash is the odd cousin in the family. It has a crunchy texture and strangely resembles spaghetti strands when cooked. Spaghetti squash will blend with the flavors of whatever it is cooked with, so experiment by combining it with different kinds of oils, cheeses, herbs and other vegetables.

ABUNDANT
SQUASH

There is an old saying in New England that the only time of year you need to lock your car doors is in August, when squash is in season. A generous neighborly gesture is to leave a full bag of zucchini on the seat of a car or a doorstep, when no one is around to politely refuse to accept it!

NOTE FROM DIANE—Composting is a simple step you can take to reduce the amount of garbage that you send to the landfill, and at the same time produce a nutrient-rich substance to add to your garden, potted plants or lawn. Composting is as simple as having a container on the counter to hold food scraps (egg shells, fruit or vegetable peelings, coffee grounds) that has a tight-fitting lid and is easy to clean. Empty this into a larger bin outdoors, and turn the compost occasionally. I use two large bins instead of one; I fill one until it is two-thirds full, then move to the next while the first one "cooks". Even if you don't have access to a yard, there are small composters available that work right in your kitchen!

BRAISED CABBAGE WITH RED WINE AND CURRANTS

Approximately 4 cups green cabbage,
   thinly sliced

¾ cup onion, chopped

⅓ cup dried currants

⅓ cup red wine

1 ½ tablespoons brown sugar

1 tablespoon olive oil

1 tablespoon black currant vinegar

½ teaspoon dried cinnamon

¼ teaspoon salt

Serves six

♦ Preheat the oven to 375 ºF.

♦ In a medium bowl mix together the cabbage, onion, currants, wine, sugar, olive oil, vinegar and cinnamon.

♦ Place the mixture into a small roasting pan. Roast for 30 minutes, stirring occasionally, until cabbage is softened. Season with salt and serve.

HARVEST HINT

Simple vinegars, such as red, white or cider vinegar are rarely made locally, but you can find vinegars infused with local herbs, fruits and spices. There are some very interesting, more exotic vinegars, with balsamic being the most commonly used (and our favorite). Balsamic vinegar is made from fermented white grapes that have been aged in wooden barrels to produce sweet vinegar with the consistency of syrup. Because of the aging process, balsamic vinegar is more expensive than other types of vinegars. To keep flavors at their best, store all vinegars, tightly sealed, in a cool dark place.

Parmesan Potato Pancakes

1 ½ cups Yukon gold potatoes, grated

2 tablespoons onion, finely chopped

2 tablespoons fresh Parmesan
   cheese, grated

2 tablespoons milk

1 tablespoon whole-wheat flour

½ teaspoon fresh garlic, minced

¼ teaspoon fresh rosemary,
   finely chopped

Pinch salt and fresh ground
   black pepper

2 tablespoons canola oil

Sour cream and sun-dried tomato
   pesto, to garnish

Serves four

◆ In a large bowl combine Yukon gold potatoes, onion, Parmesan cheese, milk, flour, garlic and rosemary. Add pinch of salt and pepper. Mix well with a spoon, or your hand, and set aside.

◆ Using a nonstick sauté pan over medium heat, heat the 2 tablespoons of canola oil.

◆ Divide the potato mixture into 4 equal parts. Using your hands, flatten each portion into a pancake about a half-inch thick and place in hot oil. As you do this, lay the pancake away from you to avoid splattering the oil on yourself.

◆ Cook for 3 to 4 minutes until golden brown on the bottom.

◆ Turn over and cook the other side for about 4 minutes.

◆ Garnish with sour cream and sun-dried tomato pesto.

HARVEST HINT

The most economical way to buy local potatoes is by the bushel, but only if you can store them properly. Potatoes need to be stored in a cool, dark, well-ventilated place where the temperature is steady between 42 and 50 degrees Fahrenheit. When potatoes are not properly stored they will either sprout or spoil. Potatoes can also turn green if exposed to sunlight, which produces a naturally occurring toxin called solanine. This toxin is harmful if consumed in large quantities.

SAVORY RED BEETS

1 ½ slices bacon, minced

3 tablespoons onion, minced

1 ½ tablespoons all-purpose flour

3 cups beets, cooked, shredded
(beets may be roasted or boiled)

1 ½ tablespoons brown sugar or
maple sugar

1 ½ tablespoons white vinegar

Serves four

◆ Place the bacon in a sauté pan over medium heat, and cook until the fat is rendered and is starting to brown.

◆ Add the onions and sauté until tender, about 1 ½ minutes. Add flour and cook for 1 more minute.

◆ Add beets and cook for 3 minutes, stirring occasionally. Stir in sugar and vinegar. Continue to cook, stirring until liquid is mostly absorbed. Serve.

HARVEST HINT

We joke that bacon makes everything taste better! This smoky, salty, fatty treat should be used in small amounts to enhance the flavor of foods, as it can easily cover up the natural flavors of whatever you are cooking. When you buy bacon locally it will likely be sliced thicker than you are used to, or you may even buy it as a slab. Slab bacon has a rind that needs to be removed before slicing. Canadian bacon is cured and smoked pork loin, which is less fatty but does not have the same flavor or texture as bacon.

SIMMERED RED CABBAGE IN CIDER

1 tablespoon olive oil

¾ cup red onion, chopped

3 cups red cabbage, thinly sliced

¾ cup cider

⅛ cup red wine vinegar

⅛ teaspoon dried thyme

⅛ teaspoon paprika

⅛ teaspoon salt

⅛ teaspoon fresh ground black pepper

1 medium red apple

1 tablespoon fresh parsley, chopped

Serves six

◆ In a sauté pan, heat the olive oil over medium-high. Add the onion and cook until soft and lightly browned, about 5 minutes.

◆ Reduce the heat to low. Add the cabbage, cider, vinegar, thyme, paprika, salt and pepper. Simmer uncovered for 30 minutes.

◆ Chop the apple into quarter-inch pieces. Add the apple and parsley to the cabbage, mix and continue simmering for another 15 minutes. Serve.

HARVEST HINT

Red cabbage is sweeter tasting than the green version, and is an important winter vegetable in the Northeast because it stores so well. Cabbage is inexpensive and versatile; it can be braised, stir-fried or used raw in salads to add some crunch. Its rich red color is a beautiful addition to any winter meal.

CHEDDAR SCALLOPED POTATOES
WITH HORSERADISH

1 tablespoon olive oil

¾ cup onion, sliced

1½ tablespoons fresh garlic, chopped

¼ cup Homegrown Horseradish
   (see page 229 for recipe)

⅛ teaspoon salt

¼ teaspoon fresh ground black pepper

Olive oil for baking dish

1½ pounds potatoes, peeled
   and sliced quarter-inch thick

1½ teaspoons all-purpose flour

⅔ cup sharp cheddar cheese, grated

½ cup milk

¼ cup low fat sour cream

Serves four

◆ Preheat oven to 350 ºF.

◆ Heat 1 tablespoon of olive oil in a saucepan over medium-high heat. Add the onions to the saucepan and cook for approximately 8 minutes, or until the onions are lightly browned. Add the garlic and cook for another minute. Remove from heat.
Add the horseradish, salt and pepper to the pan and mix.

◆ Lightly oil a 1-quart casserole dish. Arrange a layer of potatoes in the casserole dish and sprinkle with ½ teaspoon of flour. On top of the potatoes arrange one-third of the onion mixture, and then one-third of the cheese, then a layer of potatoes. Repeat, reserving the last one-third of cheese.

◆ In a measuring cup mix together the milk and sour cream. Pour over the top of the potatoes, and then sprinkle with the remaining cheese.

◆ Place in the oven, uncovered, and bake for 90 minutes. Test for doneness by inserting a sharp knife into the potatoes; when ready the potatoes should be tender, and cheese should be lightly browned on top. Serve.

HARVEST HINT

Potatoes just picked from the garden are a special treat, and aren't that difficult to grow. If you have just a small amount of garden space and want to grow your own potatoes, try using an efficient-upright container that can be easily opened or tipped over. Start with soil on the bottom and then add more soil as the potatoes grow upright. At the end of the season remove the soil, collect the potatoes and enjoy!

Creamy Risotto with Sweet Potato and Parmesan

2 tablespoons butter

¼ cup onion, finely chopped

¾ cup Arborio rice

2 ¼ cups Basic Chicken Stock
  (see page 61 for recipe)

¾ cup sweet potato, peeled and
  shredded

2 tablespoons Parmesan cheese, grated

Fresh ground black pepper

Serves four

◆ Heat a saucepan over medium heat, add butter and melt. Add the onions and sauté until onions are tender, about 2 minutes.

◆ Add rice and sauté for 1 minute, then add one-third of the chicken stock.

◆ Stirring continuously, cook for 10 minutes or until liquid is absorbed.

◆ Add the next one-third of stock, and repeat step 3.

◆ Add the last third of the stock and the sweet potato, and cook until rice is creamy and potato is tender. Add the Parmesan cheese and pepper, stir and serve.

HARVEST HINT

Stirring the rice every few minutes releases the starches and creates a creamy texture to the rice. You can substitute the sweet potato with butternut squash or even pumpkin.

SWEET ENDINGS

Dessert can be a decadent end to the meal, or a light finishing touch, depending on what's on the menu. We share many recipes that are light, fruit-based, and take advantage of whatever harvest is available. Many of the recipes are flexible depending on what fruits can be found at the market, and can be prepared with stored fruit in the colder seasons. We have included a guide *(A Year of Seasonal Foods)* and we encourage you to take the time during the bountiful summer months to preserve some of your favorite fruits. You can make many of these desserts by using or substituting with the fruits you have stored, creating wonderful treats to share with loved ones on cold winter nights.

Sweet Endings

WINTER

Minted Currant Tart with Gingersnap Crust

Crust

Butter for pan

1 ½ cups gingersnaps, ground

3 tablespoons butter, melted

1 tablespoon maple sugar

Filling

1 whole egg plus 1 egg yolk

1 tablespoon all-purpose flour

¾ cup mascarpone cheese

2 teaspoons fresh mint, finely chopped

1 tablespoon honey

2 cups fresh red currants (or frozen)

Serves eight

◆ Preheat the oven to 350 °F. Lightly grease a 10-inch round springform pan.

◆ In a medium bowl mix together the ground gingersnaps, butter and maple sugar. Spread the mixture evenly in the pan, pressing down firmly. Bake in the oven for 10 minutes, then let cool completely.

◆ In a medium bowl add the egg, egg yolk and flour, and whisk together. Add the cheese, mint and honey, and whisk together until smooth.

◆ Spread the currants out evenly in the pan, on top of the crust. Slowly pour the cheese mixture evenly over the currants.

◆ Bake for approximately 45 minutes, until the edges begin to lightly brown, and the filling is firm. Let cool, remove the outside of the pan, and slice as you would a pie.

HARVEST HINT

Mint is so much more than a green leafy garnish. Mint leaves have a very strong, distinct mint aroma. There are many varieties of mint, with some of the more popular types being spearmint, peppermint, chocolate and sage mint. Mint is a hardy perennial plant that is quick and easy to grow; just snip off what you need. You can dry the leaves to brew your own tea or use them to infuse mint flavor into many different types of foods, including salads, meats or desserts.

SWEET SPRING CRUMBLE

Rhubarb Filling

3 cups rhubarb, washed and cut into
  1-inch pieces

2 cups strawberries, washed,
  stemmed and cut in half

⅓ cup brown sugar

1 tablespoon cornstarch

1 tablespoon lemon juice

1 teaspoon ground cinnamon

Oat Crumble

1 cup rolled oats

¾ cup whole-wheat flour

½ cup all-purpose flour

⅓ cup brown sugar

1 teaspoon ground cinnamon

½ cup canola oil or melted butter

Serves six

◆ Preheat oven to 350 °F.

◆ Combine the rhubarb, strawberries, brown sugar, cornstarch, lemon juice and cinnamon in a large bowl and mix well. Let sit for 30 minutes so that the fruit combines with the sugar.

◆ To make the crumble, in a large bowl combine the rolled oats, whole-wheat and all-purpose flours, brown sugar and cinnamon and mix together with your hands until evenly blended. Make a small well in the middle of the flour mixture and pour in the canola oil or butter. With a spoon mix until the oil or butter is absorbed by the flour mixture. Using your hands rub, the mixture between your fingers until small lumps start to form.

◆ In a 1 ½-quart round casserole dish, evenly spread out the fruit mixture and shake the dish to settle the fruit. Spread the crumb topping evenly on top of the fruit.

◆ Bake for 20 to 35 minutes, until lightly browned. The baking time for this recipe will vary depending upon the type of baking dish you use. If you prefer to use a ceramic dish, it will take a few minutes longer. Let cool slightly and serve.

HARVEST HINT

Rhubarb and strawberries are the first fruits of the spring season, and so they are often used together. The tartness of the rhubarb is graciously offset by the sweet strawberries in this fresh spring dessert.

FRESH PEACHES WITH MASCARPONE AND BLACKBERRY COULIS

2 fresh peaches

4 teaspoons butter

8 large fresh mint leaves, chopped

½ cup fresh blackberries

¼ cup mascarpone cheese

1 tablespoon maple syrup

Serves four

◆ Cut the peaches in half and remove the pits. Peel each half. Place the peaches in a medium size bowl.

◆ Place the butter in a small glass bowl and microwave briefly, just until the butter melts. Add the chopped mint to the butter and mix.

◆ Add the warm butter mixture to the peaches, and toss to coat the peaches lightly. Set aside.

◆ In a food processor, purée the blackberries until smooth. Pour through a fine sieve to remove the seeds. Place the purée in a small saucepan, and cook over medium heat for approximately 2 minutes, stirring. The purée should be slightly thickened when ready, but be careful to not let it burn.

◆ In a small bowl mix together the mascarpone cheese and maple syrup.

◆ Heat the grill to 350 °F. Grill the peaches on both sides until just tender, and grill marks are visible.

◆ To serve, place one peach half in a fruit dish, place the mascarpone mixture into the hollow of the peach and drip the blackberry coulis over the top. Serve.

HARVEST HINT

Even though this dessert includes luscious mascarpone cheese, it is still quite light tasting, and is an easy finish to a late summer meal. If you preserve peaches, you can serve this recipe in the winter by skipping the grilling step and using frozen blackberries, blueberries or strawberries to make the coulis.

Strawberry Daiquiri Sorbet

Simple Syrup

1 teaspoon orange peel, freshly grated

1 teaspoon lemon peel, freshly grated

¾ cup sugar

¾ cup water

Strawberry Mixture

8 cups strawberries, stems removed

¼ cup light rum

2 tablespoons water

¼ cup fresh lime juice
   (or juice from 2 limes)

Serves six generously

◆ To make the simple syrup, combine the orange peel, lemon peel, sugar and water in a small saucepan and bring to a boil. Cook until sugar is completely dissolved. Remove from heat. Refrigerate until thoroughly cooled (overnight is best).

◆ Combine the strawberries, rum and water in a blender, and purée until smooth.

◆ Strain the fruit through a fine mesh sieve to remove the seeds. It should yield about 5 ½ cups of liquid.

◆ Add the simple syrup and lime juice to the strawberry liquid and mix. Refrigerate mixture for 2 to 3 hours.

◆ To make the ice cream, follow the instructions given for your ice cream maker. Place in a freezer-proof container and store in the freezer until ready to serve.

HARVEST HINT

Ice cream making is a fun activity for kids on a hot summer day, although it is hard for them to wait for the sweet treat at the end! Plan ahead and keep some simple syrup on hand in the fridge or freezer for those days when the kids are looking for something to do. The lure of making ice cream after a hot day of picking fresh fruit will certainly encourage the kids to be productive, and the flavor of just-picked fruit will make the ice cream unbeatable. You can substitute the strawberries in this recipe with raspberries or blackberries, depending on the summer season.

BLUEBERRY SOUR CREAM GRANOLA TART

Granola Crust

6 tablespoons butter

6 tablespoons sugar

2 teaspoons vanilla

1½ cups rolled oats

4 tablespoons all-purpose flour

1 cup pecans, finely chopped

Canola oil for pan

Tart Filling

1 egg

3 tablespoons all-purpose flour

2 tablespoons sugar

1 cup sour cream

1 cup plain yogurt

⅛ teaspoon nutmeg

1 ½ cups fresh blueberries (or frozen)

Serves eight to ten

◆ In a small saucepan melt the butter over low heat. Add sugar and vanilla, and blend well. Remove from heat.

◆ In a medium bowl combine oats, flour and pecans. Mix well.

◆ Add the butter mixture, and mix until it is completely blended and the butter is absorbed by the oats.

◆ Lightly oil a 12-inch by 1-inch round tart pan. Add the granola crust to the pan and, using your hands, form a shell by pressing down and outward towards the sides of the pan. Form the sides of the crust up to the top of the tart pan.

◆ Preheat the oven to 375 ºF.

◆ To make the tart filling, in a medium-size bowl, combine the egg, flour and sugar and whisk together until smooth. Add the sour cream, yogurt and nutmeg, and whisk together until smooth and creamy.

◆ Fold the blueberries into the sour cream mixture. Fill the shell with the blueberry mixture and spread evenly with a spatula.

◆ Bake in the oven for 40 minutes. The custard should be thick when ready. Let rest for 15 minutes, then remove rim and serve.

HARVEST HINT

This recipe can also be made with frozen blueberries, so pick as many as you can when they are in season and store in the freezer in airtight bags. Frozen blueberries are easy and convenient; just scoop them out of the bag and use in desserts, cereal or on their own.

Buckwheat Crêpes with Maple Yogurt and Plums

Crêpes

¾ cup milk

¼ cup buckwheat flour

¼ teaspoon salt

4 teaspoons butter

Crêpe Filling

½ cup strained yogurt

1 tablespoon maple butter

Plums

2 tablespoons butter

2 tablespoons maple sugar

2 cups fresh plums, sliced

2 tablespoons dark rum

Serves four

◆ To make the crêpes, in a small bowl mix together the milk, flour and salt, and stir well to form a batter. Using a crêpe pan or small nonstick pan, melt 1 teaspoon of butter over medium heat. When the butter is bubbling, place just enough batter to thinly cover the bottom of the pan. Cook until the crêpe is lightly browned and curling up on the sides. Turn the crêpe over and continue to cook until both sides are browned. Repeat until batter is finished. Let the crêpes cool. Depending on the size of your crêpe pan you may get one or two extra crêpes, and you can save them for breakfast the next day.

◆ In a small bowl combine the yogurt and maple butter. Stir to blend and set aside.

◆ To prepare the plums, in a sauté pan over medium heat, stir together the butter and sugar until melted. Add the plums and cook until the plums are tender. Add the rum and light with a match; the rum should burn for just a few seconds and extinguish itself.

◆ Arrange each crêpe on a serving plate, with the browned side of the crêpe on the bottom. Spread one quarter of the yogurt mixture on each of the crêpes. Fold each crêpe in half, forming a half moon shape. Divide the plums equally on top of each crêpe. Serve.

HARVEST HINT

Buckwheat flour has been grown and harvested in Quebec for many generations, and buckwheat pancakes have traditionally been served with molasses and butter for breakfast in many Northeastern homes. Buckwheat flour has a nutty, full flavor, and contains dark black flecks. It has twice the fiber content of all-purpose flour, so it is a nutritious substitute for at least part of the flour called for in other recipes.

Summer Cherry Cornmeal Cobbler

Cherry Filling

Butter for pan

5 cups fresh sweet cherries (or frozen)

2 tablespoons maple syrup

2 tablespoons whole-wheat flour

1 tablespoon black currant liqueur

Cobbler topping

½ cup all-purpose flour

¼ cup whole-wheat flour

½ cup cornmeal

1 tablespoon granulated sugar

1 tablespoon maple sugar

2 teaspoons baking powder

½ teaspoon baking soda

¼ teaspoon salt

2 tablespoons butter, softened

¾ cup buttermilk

1 teaspoon vanilla extract

Ice cream (optional)

◆ Preheat the oven to 400 °F. Lightly grease a 2-quart baking pan. In a medium bowl mix together the cherries, maple syrup, whole-wheat flour and liqueur. Spread the cherry filling out evenly in the greased pan.

◆ To prepare the cobbler topping, combine the all-purpose and whole-wheat flours, cornmeal, granulated and maple sugars, baking powder, baking soda and salt in a large bowl. Mix together with a fork. Cut the butter into the dry ingredients.

◆ Add the buttermilk and vanilla extract to the flour mixture, and mix lightly to form the dough.

◆ Drop spoonfuls of the dough onto the cherries. Bake for 40 minutes or until the cobbler topping is lightly browned.

◆ To serve spoon the cobbler onto individual plates. Eat the cobbler just by itself, or top with a local or homemade vanilla ice cream.

Serves eight

HARVEST HINT

There are plenty of cherries available locally to eat fresh and freeze for the winter. Wash, stem and pit the cherries (it is easy work with a cherry pitter). Spread the cherries out on baking sheets, and place in the freezer. Once frozen, place them in a freezer bag and remove as much of the air as possible. Use this freezing method with any berries.

PUMPKIN BREAD PUDDING

5 cups crusty Italian bread, 1-inch cubed
(you can use whole-wheat bread
or any combination of leftover bread)

2 ¼ cups 1% milk

1 cup fresh pumpkin purée

3 large eggs

½ cup sugar

1 teaspoon vanilla extract

⅛ teaspoon salt

½ teaspoon nutmeg

½ teaspoon cinnamon

Crunchy Pumpkin Seed Brittle
(see page 200 for recipe)

Heavy cream and honey, for garnish

Serves eight

◆ Spread the bread cubes out on a cookie sheet, and let dry on the counter for 2 hours.

◆ Preheat oven to 325 ºF. Place the bread cubes in a 2-quart round baking dish.

◆ In a medium bowl mix together the milk, pumpkin, eggs, sugar, vanilla, salt, nutmeg and cinnamon. Pour this mixture over the bread cubes. Let soak for 10 minutes, occasionally pushing down any bread that rises to the top.

◆ Place the baking dish into a large, 2-inch deep pan. Fill the larger pan with water, at least 1-inch deep.

◆ Bake for 60 minutes or until slightly firm and lightly browned on top. Let cool before serving. Serve with a piece or two of Crunchy Pumpkin Seed Brittle and a dollop of heavy cream with honey.

HARVEST HINT

Pumpkin purée is simple to make, and keeps well in the freezer. To make pumpkin purée, cut the pumpkin in half and remove the seeds and fibrous strings. Place in a baking pan, cut side down. Bake in the oven at 375 ºF for 60 minutes or until soft when pierced with a knife. Let cool, and remove pulp from skin. In a food processor, purée the pulp until smooth. Portion into one-cup measures, and freeze.

CRUNCHY PUMPKIN SEED BRITTLE

Butter for pan

¾ cup sugar

¾ cup maple syrup

2 tablespoons butter

2 tablespoons water

¾ cup pumpkin seeds, roasted

¼ teaspoon baking soda

Candy thermometer

◆ Preheat the oven to 250 ºF. Grease a large cookie sheet with butter and set aside.

◆ In a medium saucepan, combine the sugar, maple syrup, butter and water. Heat over medium-low, stirring frequently, until the mixture comes to a boil.

◆ Cook over medium-low heat, without stirring, until the mixture reaches 260 ºF registered on a candy thermometer. At this point, place the pumpkin seeds on a separate baking sheet and place in the oven to warm. Do not let the seeds burn.

◆ When the mixture reaches 280 ºF stir in the warmed pumpkin seeds. Continue to cook, stirring, until the mixture reaches 300 ºF. At that time, remove from heat and quickly stir in the baking soda. Quickly pour the mixture out onto the greased cookie sheet and let cool thoroughly.

◆ When ready, break into pieces and serve. This brittle is excellent served with Pumpkin Bread Pudding (See page 199.)

HARVEST HINT

Brittle is one of the simplest forms of candy. For hundreds of years there has been some type of brittle produced, but only in more recent times have they been commonly found in American cookbooks. There are many versions of this simple recipe, but we suggest using syrups like honey, maple syrup and molasses, and other local ingredients such as pumpkin seeds, sunflower seeds and walnuts.

ISLAND APPLE CAKE

Butter for pan

2 tablespoons butter

2 cups fresh apples, peeled and cubed

1 tablespoon dark brown sugar

⅓ cup butter

1 cup granulated sugar

2 eggs

1 pinch salt

1 tablespoon baking powder

1½ cups all-purpose flour

½ cup whole-wheat flour

1 teaspoon vanilla extract

½ cup milk

½ cup walnuts, chopped

Serves eight

◆ Preheat the oven to 350 °F. Lightly grease a 7-inch by 11-inch baking pan with butter.

◆ In a sauté pan over medium heat, melt the 2 tablespoons of butter. Add the apples and sauté for 15 minutes. During the last minute of cooking, mix in the brown sugar. Remove from heat and let cool.

◆ Using an electric mixer, cream the ⅓ cup butter and granulated sugar together. Scrape the sides of the bowl down.

◆ Add the eggs, and cream for 2 minutes.

◆ In a separate bowl, add the salt and baking powder to the all-purpose and whole-wheat flours, and whisk together with a fork.

◆ Add the vanilla to the milk. Alternate adding the milk and the flour mixture to the egg mixture, until a smooth batter is formed.

◆ Fold in the apples and walnuts, and pour evenly into the greased baking pan.

◆ Bake for 35 to 45 minutes, until an inserted toothpick comes out clean. Serve topped with a small amount of Apple Cider Syrup (see recipe in Harvest Hint below).

HARVEST HINT

We consider Apple Cider Syrup the "other Vermont syrup". Make syrup by combining 3 cups apple cider and ½ cup sugar in a small saucepan. Cook over medium-high heat for 30 to 45 minutes, until reduced to syrup. When ready, it should be quite thick but still liquid enough to pour easily (like maple syrup). For a delicious tea substitute, combine 2 tablespoons of syrup, a dash of ground cinnamon and a cup of boiling water, and stir.

CLAIRE'S RASPBERRY UPSIDE-DOWN CAKE

Butter for pan

1 tablespoon granulated sugar

5 cups fresh raspberries
  (or 6 cups frozen)

⅓ cup butter, softened

1 cup granulated sugar

2 eggs

2 cups all-purpose flour

1 tablespoon baking powder

1 pinch salt

1 teaspoon vanilla extract

¾ cup milk

Serves eight

◆ Preheat the oven to 350 °F. Lightly grease a 7-inch by 11-inch baking pan.

◆ Stir the 1 tablespoon of sugar into the raspberries, and spoon the raspberries into the bottom of the baking pan, spreading them out evenly.

◆ Using an electric mixer, cream the butter and 1 cup granulated sugar together.

◆ Add the eggs to the butter mixture and cream for 2 mintues.

◆ In a separate bowl, combine the flour, baking powder and salt and whisk together using a fork.

◆ Add the vanilla to the milk. Alternate adding the milk and the flour mixture to the egg mixture, until a smooth batter is formed. Scrape the sides of the bowl during mixing.

◆ Pour the batter evenly over the raspberries.

◆ Bake for 45 minutes. To serve, spoon into a bowl, turning over so that the berries are on top.

NOTE FROM DIANE —This recipe comes from my husband's Aunt Claire, who lives in Quebec. She has picked raspberries from her own garden for decades. She shares her harvest with family by making this recipe, and we know that we can count on this treat when we visit her in late August. She serves it with a touch of fresh cream on top. Feel free to substitute the raspberries with any fresh berry in season. If using frozen berries for this recipe, add an extra cup of fruit.

CURRANT CARROT CAKE
WITH MAPLE WHIP

Cake Batter

Canola oil for pan

½ cup butter

½ cup brown sugar

5 eggs

2 cups carrots, grated

1 cup dried currants

1 cup maple syrup

½ cup applesauce

2 ½ tablespoons fresh ginger, chopped

1 ½ cups all-purpose flour

½ cup whole-wheat flour

1 tablespoon baking powder

1 tablespoon cinnamon

1 teaspoon baking soda

1 teaspoon salt

1 teaspoon ground nutmeg

Topping

⅔ cup heavy cream

1 tablespoon maple butter

Serves twelve

◆ Preheat the oven to 350 °F. Lightly oil a 13-by 9-inch baking pan.

◆ Using an electric mixer, cream the butter and sugar in a large bowl.

◆ Add the eggs and cream for 2 minutes. Add the carrots, currants, syrup, applesauce and ginger, and mix well. In a separate bowl, stir together the all-purpose and whole-wheat flours, baking powder, cinnamon, baking soda, salt and nutmeg.

◆ Add the dry ingredients to the butter mixture and mix thoroughly.

◆ Pour batter into the oiled baking pan and place in the preheated oven. Bake for 30 to 40 minutes, or until an inserted toothpick comes out clean.

◆ Using an electric mixer, whip the cream and maple butter together until stiff. Top each piece of cake with a dollop of maple whipped cream.

NOTE FROM DIANE—Currants are one of the first spring fruits to harvest in the Northeast, ripening in June. Currants are often overlooked, but I think that they are an interesting addition to both the yard and the kitchen. They are very easy to grow and since currants grow in clusters they are also easy to harvest. My family always had currants growing in the yard (both red and white) so I have harvested them all my life. It is certainly easier work as an adult, since a hot day in June or early July is a difficult time for kids to pick anything!

Maple Oatmeal Pecan Cookies
with Dark Chocolate

¾ cup canola oil

1 ¼ cup brown sugar

1 whole egg, beaten well

4 tablespoons maple syrup

1 tablespoon ground cinnamon

1 teaspoon ground nutmeg

1 tablespoon vanilla extract

1 ½ teaspoons baking soda

¼ teaspoon salt

1¾ cup whole-wheat flour

1¼ cups rolled oats

1 ¼ cups pecans, chopped

1 cup dried cranberries

4 ounces dark chocolate,
   finely chopped

Makes 3 dozen cookies

◆ Preheat oven to 350 ºF.

◆ Combine the canola oil, brown sugar, egg, maple syrup, cinnamon, nutmeg, vanilla, baking soda and salt in a large bowl. Mix until well blended and smooth. Add the whole-wheat flour, rolled oats, pecans, cranberries and dark chocolate. Mix until a dough is formed and all ingredients are well blended.

◆ Spoon out on a greased cookie sheet, dropping dough about the size of a silver dollar.

◆ Bake for 15 to 17 minutes. Remove from oven and place cookies on a wire rack; let set for 5 minutes. These cookies are delicious eaten warm or cooled to room temperature. Store in a cookie tin.

HARVEST HINT

Cookies don't have to be a sinful treat. When made with wholesome ingredients like whole-wheat flour, nuts, dried fruit (and yes, even dark chocolate), cookies are a sensible and delicious dessert choice. When eating sweets the key is moderation, and one or two of these satisfying cookies will be plenty.

"Vegetables are the food of the earth;

fruit seems to be more the food

of the heavens."

— Sepal Felicivant

Winter Holiday Trifle

Custard

2 cups whole milk

6 large egg yolks

⅓ cup sugar

Dash salt

1 teaspoon vanilla extract

Blueberry filling

2 cups frozen blueberries

1 tablespoon sugar

Apple filling

2 medium apples

1 tablespoon butter

1 tablespoon brown sugar

Strawberry Smash, thawed

(see page 220 for recipe)

1 Yellow Farmer's Cake

(see page 208 for recipe)

2 tablespoons brandy

1 cup heavy cream

Serves eight to ten

◆ Bring the milk just to boil, and remove from heat.

◆ In a medium-sized bowl, whisk together the egg yolks, sugar, and salt.

◆ Whisk the heated milk into the egg mixture, and return the whole mixture to the saucepan.

◆ Cook over low heat, whisking constantly until custard is thickened. When ready it should be thick enough to coat the back of a spoon. Remove from heat, stir in the vanilla and refrigerate.

◆ Over medium heat in a small saucepan, combine the blueberries and sugar and stir regularly until just boiling. Remove from heat and set aside to cool.

◆ Cube the apples. Over medium-high heat, melt the butter and brown sugar in a saucepan. Add the apples and sauté for 5 minutes or until lightly browned. Set aside to cool.

◆ Cut the cake horizontally into three layers.

◆ Whip the cream and set aside.

◆ In a large trifle bowl or other large glass bowl, layer the trifle as follows:

—One third custard
—First layer of cake
—1 tablespoon of brandy
—All of the blueberry mixture
—Second layer of cake
—Remaining custard
—All of the apple mixture
—Last layer of cake
—1 tablespoon brandy
—All of the Strawberry Smash
—Whipped cream

◆ Refrigerate up to several hours, until ready to serve.

YELLOW FARMER'S CAKE

Canola oil and flour for pan

1 ¾ cups all-purpose flour

¼ cup cornstarch

1 teaspoon baking soda

¼ teaspoon salt

1 tablespoon vanilla extract

¼ cup canola oil

¼ cup 2% milk

2 tablespoons butter, melted

5 whole eggs

1 cup sugar

Serves eight to ten

◆ Preheat oven to 350 ºF.

◆ Lightly oil and flour a 10-inch round cake pan.

◆ Combine the flour, cornstarch, baking soda and salt and sift twice. Set aside.

◆ In a small bowl combine the vanilla extract, canola oil, milk and butter. Set aside.

◆ In a separate bowl combine the eggs and sugar and, using an electric mixer, beat for 2 minutes on medium speed. Then beat for 5 minutes on high speed. After 5 minutes the egg batter should be 5 times the original volume and have firm peaks.

◆ Add one-third of the flour mixture into the egg batter and gently fold in.

◆ Add another third of the flour mixture into the egg batter. Add half the milk and oil mixture and gently fold in. Add the remaining flour mixture into the egg batter, add the remaining milk and oil mixture and gently fold in. Pour the batter into the oiled and floured pan.

◆ Bake in the oven for 25 to 28 minutes. The cake should be golden brown on top and spring back slightly when touched. A toothpick inserted in the cake should come out clean. Remove the cake from the oven and let rest for 15 minutes. Remove from cake pan and let cool on a wire rack.

HARVEST HINT

Farm eggs come in different sizes and colors, which make them lovely to look at, but sometimes challenging to use. In general, recipes are based on large-size eggs, so pay special attention to the size of eggs in recipes like pasta or cakes, and try to choose the egg that would be closest to a large-size egg.

OATMEAL MAPLE TRAIL BARS

1 ½ cups rolled oats

¾ cup pecans, chopped

¾ cup dried fruit (cranberries, apples, cherries, blueberries)

¼ cup plus 2 tablespoons whole-wheat flour

¼ cup canola oil

6 tablespoons maple syrup

4 tablespoons ground flax seed

3 tablespoons maple sugar

2 tablespoons apple cider or water

2 teaspoons white sesame seeds

1 teaspoon vanilla

Makes 15 bars

◆ Preheat the oven to 375 ºF.

◆ In a mixing bowl combine the oats, pecans, dried fruit, whole-wheat flour, canola oil, maple syrup, flax seed, maple sugar, cider, sesame seeds and vanilla.

◆ Mix on low speed until the mixture is blended together and becomes stiff, about 2 minutes.

◆ Place the mixture into a lightly oiled 9-inch by 7-inch pan. Spread the mixture out evenly across the pan and smooth the top. With a knife cut the mixture into bars about that are 5-inches by 3-inches, leaving ⅛-inch between bars.

◆ Bake in the oven for 19 to 21 minutes until bars are lightly golden brown around the edges.

◆ Remove from oven and set aside to cool for 30 minutes. Remove bars from pan with a spatula. They should separate easily into bars. Store in a cookie tin or freeze.

HARVEST HINT

Flax seeds contain omega-3 fats, fiber, zinc, iron, vitamin E and calcium. To make the nutrients in flax available for your body to use, grind the seeds in a food processor or coffee grinder. Grind only as much as you need for a recipe, as the whole seeds store better. To prevent spoilage store seeds in an airtight container in the freezer.

EXOTIC INGREDIENTS, such as vanilla, olive oil, vinegars, spices, cocoa, tea and coffee, have been imported and traded for centuries. Since these foods are often used in small quantities, buying them has less economic significance than importing other items such as produce, meats and cheeses. Our approach is to buy local whenever possible,

Simmered Harvest Fruit
with Minted Ricotta

Simmered Fruit

1 inch vanilla bean

1 cup dried apples (if full rings,
    cut in half)

½ cup dried cherries

1 ¼ cups port

2 tablespoons fresh orange juice

1 teaspoon orange peel

1 tablespoon brown sugar

¼ teaspoon ground cinnamon

⅛ teaspoon ground clove

Ricotta Topping

1 cup firm ricotta cheese

1 tablespoon fresh mint, chopped

Fresh mint leaves, to garnish

Serves four

◆ Place the vanilla bean in a cheesecloth and tie it closed. If you don't have cheesecloth, you can use a tea infuser instead.

◆ In a small saucepan combine the apples, cherries, port, orange juice, peel, brown sugar, cinnamon and clove. Add the vanilla bean, and bring to a boil. Immediately reduce heat to low. Simmer for 45 minutes, until liquid is reduced to ½ cup.

◆ In a small bowl, mix the ricotta with the chopped mint and refrigerate while the fruit is simmering.

◆ Remove the vanilla bean from the fruit mixture, and divide the fruit evenly into four dessert bowls.

◆ Evenly divide the ricotta on top of the fruit. Garnish each with a sprig of fresh mint. Serve.

HARVEST HINT

Since there is limited availability of fresh local fruit in the Northeast during the winter months, look for locally grown and dried fruit in your local markets, or dry them yourself during the harvest season. There is an increasing variety of dried fruits available, including cranberries, blueberries, cherries and apples.

CHOCOLATE SOUR MILK CAKE

1 ½ cups sugar

6 tablespoons butter

2 cups all-purpose flour

1 cup cocoa powder

2 tablespoons baking powder

⅛ teaspoon salt

1 ½ cups soured milk

2 whole eggs, beaten

2 teaspoons vanilla extract

1 cup boiling water

Canola oil and flour for pan

Whipped heavy cream and
   strawberries, for garnish

Serves eight to ten

◆ Preheat the oven to 350 ºF.

◆ Using an electric mixer, beat the sugar and butter until smooth and creamy.

◆ In a separate bowl sift together the flour, cocoa powder, baking powder and salt.

◆ Add the sifted flour mixture to the sugar mixture and lightly blend.

◆ In a separate bowl, combine the soured milk, egg and vanilla extract and mix lightly to blend.

◆ Slowly add the milk mixture to the flour and sugar, continually mixing until well blended.

◆ Add the boiling water and mix on low speed for 1 minute. Scrape down the sides of the bowl and mix for 1 more minute.

◆ Lightly oil and flour 9-inch by 10-inch rectangular pan or a 12-inch round pan. Scrape cake batter into the cake pan and bake for 30 to 40 minutes. Test the cake by inserting a toothpick in center; the toothpick should come out clean when the cake is ready. The cake should also spring back when touched in the center. Let cool. Cut and serve cake with whipped cream and strawberries. If making this dessert in the summer, use fresh strawberries as mentioned. If making it in the winter, use the Strawberry Smash recipe as a topping.

HARVEST HINT

To make soured milk, stir in 1 ½ tablespoons of white vinegar or lemon juice to 1 ½ cups of whole milk. Let stand at room temperature for 10 minutes, then use in this recipe.

TRULY CHOCOLATE ICE CREAM

1 ½ cups sugar

1 cup cocoa powder

2 cups light cream

2 cups 2% milk

1 tablespoon vanilla extract

4 egg yolks

Makes several cups

◆ Combine the sugar and cocoa together in a bowl and mix well.

◆ In a separate bowl combine the cream, milk, vanilla extract and egg yolks. Whisk until completely blended.

◆ Add the cream mixture to the sugar and cocoa, and mix well.

◆ In a 4-quart saucepan, heat the cream and cocoa mixture over medium heat, bringing slowly to a boil. When small bubbles form, reduce the heat to a simmer and cook until the mixture is slightly thickened (about 5 minutes). Stir constantly with a whisk, being careful not to let the mixture burn.

◆ Refrigerate the custard overnight and then follow the instructions for your ice cream maker to make the ice cream.

HARVEST HINT

For additional flavor and texture in any homemade ice cream add nuts, dried cranberries, cherries, granola or dark chocolate chunks. Add about one cup total of ingredients (chilled) and stir into the mixture at the very end.

FILLING THE PANTRY

There are many different ways to savor the summer harvest throughout the year. You can use different methods of preserving such as drying, canning, vacuum-sealing, and freezing foods, including herbs, vegetables, meats, grains, tomatoes and other fruits. In Filling the Pantry you will find some of our favorite recipes to help you store your summer harvest to enjoy all winter, and into the spring. Preserving does not have to be complicated, but it can be time consuming and is worth it in the end. Just remember to start with the freshest ingredients available in season. We have included a guide to key ingredients to preserve for a year of seasonal recipes. Life is a harvest of good food, so enjoy the best of your local farmers' market all year long.

Filling the Pantry

STRAWBERRY SMASH

4 cups fresh strawberries
(about ½ pound)

4 tablespoons sugar

1 teaspoon vanilla extract

3 pint jars

Makes 3 pints

◆ In a medium saucepan, mix the strawberries, sugar and vanilla. Cook over medium-high heat, mashing strawberries lightly with a potato masher. Cook, stirring occasionally for 7 to 8 minutes or until moderately thickened. Remove from heat and let cool.

◆ Pour strawberry mixture into pint jars. Freeze for later use. Strawberry Smash will keep in the freezer for the winter.

HARVEST HINT

Make this recipe in June and early July, when strawberries are abundant. This recipe is a useful way to store strawberries for later seasons. By lightly processing the berries you can avoid any freezer burn on the fruit. Use this strawberry mixture throughout the fall and winter added to plain yogurt, over pound cake or in the Winter Holiday Trifle recipe. The pint jars go quickly but are a good size to keep the mixture fresh while in the refrigerator. This recipe may be doubled.

Fresh Basil Pesto

2 cups fresh basil leaves

½ cup olive oil

3 fresh garlic cloves, peeled

¼ cup pine nuts

¼ cup Parmesan cheese, grated

◆ In a food processor mix the basil, olive oil, garlic and pine nuts.

◆ Process until smooth.

◆ Add the cheese to the processor and pulse until well blended. Use fresh or freeze for later use.

HARVEST HINT

To preserve pesto, freeze in an ice cube tray. Once frozen, remove from tray and store in freezer bags.
Try any of these pestos spread on top of baked or grilled fish and chicken, as a sandwich spread, tossed with pasta, on pizza or as a marinade.

Sunflower Basil Pesto

3 fresh garlic cloves, peeled

½ cup sunflower seeds, raw, unsalted, shelled

¼ teaspoon salt

⅛ teaspoon fresh ground black pepper

2 tablespoons fresh lemon juice

½ cup olive oil

5 cups fresh basil leaves

◆ In a food processor mix the garlic, sunflower seeds, salt, pepper, lemon juice and olive oil. Process until seeds are chopped finely but not completely ground.

◆ Add half the basil leaves and process briefly.

◆ Add the remaining basil leaves and mix until chopped, but not completely puréed.

◆ Use fresh or freeze for later use.

HARVEST HINT

If you don't have a refrigerator thermometer we recommend that you buy one. A correctly functioning refrigerator will result in less wasted food from spoilage, help ensure that your food is safe and save energy. Place the thermometer on the top shelf, towards the front. A refrigerator should maintain food at 41 °F or less, so the refrigerator temperature should be closer to 39 °F. The door is usually the warmest place in the refrigerator, so don't store highly perishable foods like milk or cheese on the door.

CILANTRO AND PUMPKIN SEED PESTO

2 fresh garlic cloves, peeled

½ cup pumpkin seeds, raw unsalted

¼ teaspoon salt

⅛ teaspoon fresh ground black pepper

2 tablespoons fresh lime juice

½ cup olive oil

4 cups fresh cilantro leaves and stems

◆ In a food processor mix the garlic, pumpkin seeds, salt, pepper, lime juice and olive oil. Process until seeds are finely chopped but not completely ground.

◆ Add half the cilantro and process briefly.

◆ Add the remaining cilantro leaves and mix until chopped, but not completely puréed. Use fresh or freeze for later.

HARVEST HINT

Ample freezer space is needed if you are serious about eating locally throughout the winter. There are so many opportunities in the summer to buy or grow foods that store well in the freezer, like berries, tomatoes and many other vegetables. To ensure that your freezer is operating efficiently, keep it at least two-thirds full. As you empty it during the winter, fill it with large containers of ice so that you will have ice blocks on hand for summer outings.

PICKLED SUMMER VEGETABLES

2 yellow squash, cut in half length-wise
  and sliced ¼-inch

2 red bell peppers, cored and chopped
  into 1-inch pieces

1 green bell pepper, cored and chopped
  into 1-inch pieces

1 yellow pepper, cored and chopped
  into 1-inch pieces

1 zucchini, cut in half length-wise
  and sliced ¼-inch

1 pound pickling cucumbers,
  sliced ¼-inch (we recommend Kirby)

⅓ cup pickling salt

1 ½ quarts ice cubes

2 ½ cups white vinegar (5%)

2 cups sugar

6 garlic cloves, peeled

2 teaspoons mustard seed

1 teaspoon black peppercorns

2 fresh bay leaves

6 sprigs fresh parsley

6 pint jars

◆ In a large bowl combine the squash, peppers, zucchini and cucumbers. Stir in the salt and toss to coat. Cover with ice and refrigerate for 6 hours.

◆ Remove the ice and drain the liquid from the vegetables. In a large pot combine the vinegar, sugar, garlic, mustard seed, peppercorns and bay leaves. Bring to a boil.

◆ Add the vegetables to the vinegar mixture and quickly bring to a boil.

◆ Sterilize 6 pint-size canning jars. Using a slotted spoon, divide the vegetable mixture into the jars, assuring that there is a clove of garlic in each. Add a sprig of parsley to each jar. Using a ladle, add the liquid to fill within ½-inch of the top of each jar. Place the lids on the jars, and process in a boiling water bath for 10 minutes.

◆ Store in the pantry.

Makes 6 pints

NOTE FROM DIANE— This recipe is inspired by some pickled vegetables shared with me from a good friend, and made by his mother and grandmother. This recipe isn't quite the same, but the intent of saving fresh, crispy summer vegetables to use later in the season is the same. Generations ago, the original recipe was created by the Boulet family of Quebec.

THIRD GENERATION BREAD
AND BUTTER PICKLES

4 quarts cucumbers, sliced ¼-inch wide

6 medium onions, sliced

2 green bell peppers, chopped

3 garlic cloves, peeled

⅓ cup kosher salt

1 ½ quarts ice cubes

3 cups white vinegar (5%)

5 cups sugar

1 ½ teaspoons celery seed

1 ½ teaspoons turmeric

4 quart-size jars

Makes 4 quarts

◆ In a large pot combine the cucumbers, onions, green bell peppers and garlic. Stir in the salt and toss to coat.

◆ Cover the mixture with the ice, cover the pot and refrigerate for 3 hours.

◆ Remove the ice and drain the liquid from the cucumber mixture. Return the mixture to the pot.

◆ Add to the cucumber mixture the vinegar, sugar, celery seed and turmeric. Mix thoroughly and bring to a boil.

◆ Sterilize 4 quart-size canning jars. Using a slotted spoon, divide the cucumber mixture into the four jars. Using a ladle, add the liquid to fill within a ½-inch of the top of each jar. Place the lids on the jars, and process in a boiling water bath for 10 minutes.

NOTE FROM RICHARD—This pickle recipe came to me from my mother-in-law, who resides along the coast in southern Maine. She has been making this pickle recipe every summer for the past four decades. The original recipe came from her friends Dot and Armand, whose family had passed down this recipe for generations. They always told me that the secret to this recipe is to ice the cucumbers so that they will be crisp when they are canned. This secret will make the crunchiest pickles you have ever eaten!

Maple Blackberry Barbeque Sauce

⅔ cup red wine vinegar

½ cup maple syrup

½ cup maple sugar

½ cup onion, finely chopped

3 tablespoons fresh ginger root, minced

2 tablespoons fresh garlic, minced

1 cup fresh blackberries

3 cups ketchup (we recommend
   Richard's of Vermont)

1 cup water

½ cup soy sauce

1 tablespoon jalapeño pepper, chopped

2 teaspoons chili powder (or ½ teaspoon
   ground chipotle pepper)

2 teaspoons paprika

4 half-pint jars

Makes four half-pint jars

◆ Place the vinegar, maple syrup and maple sugar in a saucepan. Bring to a boil and add the onion, ginger and garlic. Reduce heat and simmer for 5 minutes.

◆ Purée the blackberries in a food processor. Using a fine sieve, strain out the seeds and set aside the purée.

◆ Add the ketchup, water, soy sauce, jalapeño, chili powder, paprika and the blackberry purée. Simmer for 10 to 15 minutes, until the sauce is thickened and is dark red in color. Let cool and divide into the jars. Use within a week, or freeze for later.

Note: This recipe can be made in any season using homemade ketchup, frozen blackberries and Pickled Jalapeño Peppers (p. 231).

HARVEST HINT

Locally processed foods such as jam, jellies and pickles are standard fare at any farmers' market. In recent years there has been an increase in other, more unique products such as hot sauce, Master Sauce, pickled garlic, salad dressings, salsas, marinades and sauces. These interesting products are a welcome change from some of the mass-produced items on the grocery store shelves. They add a local flavor to your favorite recipes and help support your local producers and economy.

SWEET AND SPICY CORN RELISH

2 cups cider vinegar

1 ⅓ cups red onion, chopped

1 cup granulated maple sugar

¼ cup finely chopped garlic

1 ⅓ cups red bell pepper,
  finely chopped

1 tablespoon plus 1 teaspoon
  jalapeño pepper, finely chopped

2 teaspoons kosher salt

8 cups raw fresh corn, removed
  from the cob

1 cup cilantro, finely chopped

4 pint jars

Makes four pints

◆ Heat a medium saucepan over medium-high heat and add the vinegar, onions, sugar, garlic, red pepper, jalapeño and salt. Bring to a rapid boil for 1 to 2 minutes.

◆ Add the corn and continue to boil rapidly for 2 to 3 minutes, and then remove from heat.

◆ Stir in cilantro. Refrigerate for 2 hours before serving.

◆ To preserve the relish, sterilize 4 pint-size canning jars. Using a slotted spoon, divide the vegetable mixture into the jars, filling to within ½-inch of the top of each jar. Place the lids on the jars, and process in a boiling water bath for 20 minutes. Store in the pantry.

HOMEGROWN HORSERADISH

6 ounces peeled horseradish

  (about 10 ounces unpeeled)

¼ cup water

½ teaspoon salt

1 tablespoon sugar

½ cup white vinegar

Makes approximately four half-pint jars

◆ Chop the horseradish into half-inch pieces. In a food processor, combine the horseradish, water, salt and sugar, and process until smooth.

◆ Add the vinegar and process until thoroughly mixed.

◆ Spoon into half-pint jars, and refrigerate for up to 3 weeks. Freeze the horseradish if you won't use all of it within this time.

NOTE FROM DIANE— Horseradish can be an acquired taste, as it is bitter and strong tasting. My father says that horseradish is only good if you can feel it in your sinuses, and really good if it makes you cry! The edible portion of horseradish is the root, which must be peeled before use. Be careful if you are planning to add horseradish plants to your garden, although they are low maintenance they also spread quickly.

"When we tug at a single thing in nature,
we find it attached to the rest of the world."

— *John Muir*

PICKLED JALAPEÑO PEPPERS

1 cup white vinegar

1 tablespoon pickling salt

1 cup water

8 to 10 jalapeño peppers, tops removed,
　　cored and chopped.

5 four-ounce canning jars

Makes five half-pint jars

◆ Sterilize 5 four-ounce canning jars.

◆ In a small saucepan combine vinegar, salt and water
and bring to a boil.

◆ Fill all jars with chopped pepper to about half an inch
from top of the jar.

◆ Fill the pepper-stuffed jars with the boiling vinegar mixture
to half an inch from the top of the jar. Place the lids on the jars
and process in a boiling water bath for 10 minutes.
Store in the pantry.

HARVEST HINT

To prevent burning yourself, use rubber gloves when handling hot peppers, and do not touch your skin or face with
your gloved hands. Drying hot peppers for storage is very simple, and with very little effort it will provide you with enough
peppers to last the winter. Simply rinse and towel dry a few dozen peppers, and string them using a large needle and thin
string. Hang them in a dry, well-ventilated area.

A Year of Seasonal Recipes

FOODS TO CAN

Hot Sauce*
Maple Barbeque Sauce
Pickled Jalapeño Peppers
Pickled Summer Vegetables
Strawberry Jam*
Third Generation Bread and
   Butter Pickles
Tomatoes *

FOODS TO FREEZE

Blueberries
Cherries
Chestnuts
Cranberries
Currants
Raspberries
Shell Peas
Strawberries
Tomato Juice
Tomatoes (chopped or whole)
Atomic Horseradish
Basic Chicken Stock
Chunky Fresh Tomato Basil Sauce
Chunky Roasted Tomato Soup
Eggplant Tomato Sauce
Garlic-Roasted Cherry Tomatoes
Homemade Rustic Tomato Sauce
Pesto
Pumpkin Purée
Roasted Peppers
Simple Syrup
Strawberry Smash
Vegetable Stock*

FOODS TO DRY

Apples
Assorted herbs

Cherries
Cherry Tomatoes
Cranberries
Currants
Mushrooms
Roma Tomatoes

FOODS TO STORE

Apples
Beets
Cabbage
Carrots
Celeriac
Garlic
Ginger
Kohlrabi
Onions
Parsnips
Pears
Potatoes
Rutabaga
Shallots
Tomatillos
Turnip
Winter Squash
Cornmeal
Flour – different kinds
Oats
Pumpkin Seeds
Wheat Berries
Black, Cannellini and
   Red Cranberry Beans
Honey
Maple Sugar
Maple Syrup

* Recipes not included

INDEX

INDEX

INDEX

INDEX

INDEX

the politics and practice of sustainable living

CHELSEA GREEN PUBLISHING

Chelsea Green Publishing sees books as tools for effecting cultural change and seeks to empower citizens to participate in reclaiming our global commons and become its impassioned stewards. If you enjoyed *Cooking Close to Home*, please consider these other great books related to food.

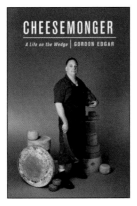

CHEESEMONGER
A Life on the Wedge
GORDON EDGAR
9781603582377
Paper • $17.95

WILD FERMENTATION
SANDOR ELLIX KATZ
9781931498234
Paperback • $25.00

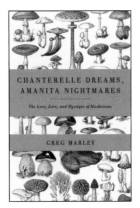

CHANTERELLE DREAMS,
AMANITA NIGHTMARES
*The Love, Lore, and
Mystique of Mushrooms*
GREG MARLEY
9781603582148
Paperback • $17.95

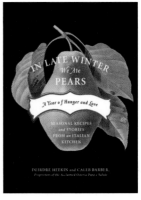

IN LATE WINTER WE ATE PEARS
A Year of Hunger and Love
DEIRDRE HEEKIN and CALEB BARBER
9781603581011
Paperback • $25.00

CHELSEA
GREEN
PUBLISHING
the politics and practice of sustainable living